OneNote in a Minute

Steps for Performing Basic Tasks in Microsoft OneNote 2010

Diane L. Martin

First Edition

My PC Associate NYC

244 Fifth Avenue, Suite 2337

New York, NY 10001

www.mypcassociate.com

OneNote in a Minute

Steps for Performing Basic Tasks in Microsoft OneNote 2010

First Edition

Diane L. Martin

My PC Associate NYC

DISCLAIMER

My PC Associate NYC takes great care to ensure the accuracy and quality of these materials. All material is provided without any warranty whatsoever, including, but not limited to, the implied warranties of merchantability or fitness for a particular purpose.

ISBN: **978-0-9856837-4-0**

My PC Associate Web site: http://www.mypcassociate.com

COMPUTE, EXCEL AND ADVANCE!

Collect the Entire

Office in a Minute Series

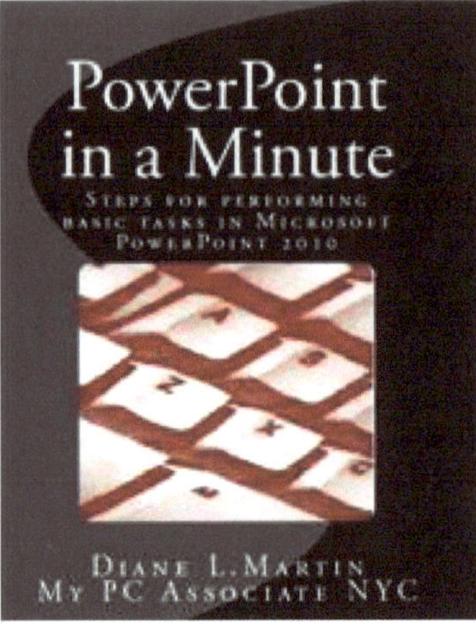

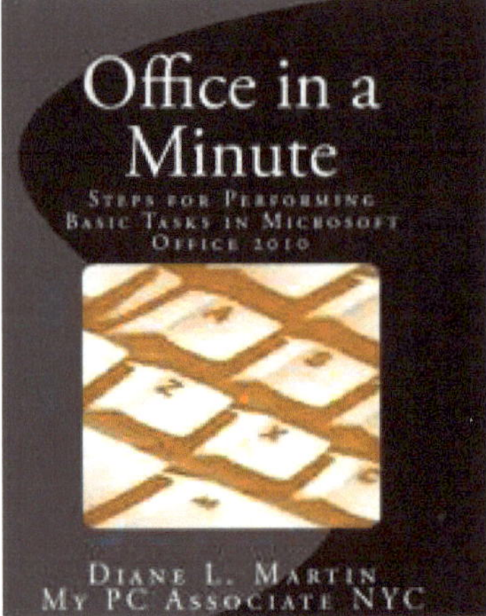

Createspace.com

Table of Contents

About this Book

The purpose of this book is to serve as a quick tutorial for those who are largely unfamiliar with Microsoft OneNote 2010. If you want to learn the most basic steps of this wonderful planning and organizer application, you have come to the right place. Through this quick tutorial, you will actually learn how to use OneNote to organize among other things, your documents, photographs, and scanned images.

To facilitate learning, we have liberally employed the use of color, screen shots, notes pages and directional arrows. We have also included more than 35 illustrations. In addition, at the start of each chapter the estimated time necessary to complete all of the tasks is listed. You may be surprised to learn that many basic tasks can be completed in less than two minutes.

There is so much you will continue to learn as you work with Microsoft OneNote. What we attempt to do here is to provide you with systematic instructions for performing basic tasks that will enable you to become a productive user.

Welcome to our tutorial. Keep in mind that proficiency comes with practice. As you continue to work with this application, your confidence, productivity and skill will improve.

The Editors

Forward

Here is Why You Will Absolutely Adore OneNote.

I have added this forward to give you an overview of the OneNote application. In my research, it became clear that among the Microsoft Office applications, OneNote appears to be the least familiar. If you have ever wanted an application that could help you finally organize all of your various digital content, you will not only adore OneNote, you will wonder how you got along without it for so long. OneNote is an electronic notebook, which actually behaves a lot like a loose-leaf binder. Moreover, like any notebook you can add both pages and sections. You can also insert videos, audio files, pictures, photographs, and text from other Microsoft applications. Additionally, you can record audio and video clips and then place them neatly into any notebook page. OneNote allows you to store this kind of data within your notebook, and then share it with friends, family or colleagues.

One of the best things about OneNote is that if you are a current Microsoft Office user, you will find the OneNote computing environment very familiar. The ribbons and tabs you have come to know in Microsoft Word, Excel and PowerPoint are also available in OneNote. In addition, you will also find familiar tools such as Format Painter, Spelling, Tables and Shapes. Distinctive new features also await you, such as Side Notes and Drawing Tools. Unfortunately, we cannot cover every feature; however, I am confident that you will nevertheless learn a great deal about this very robust application.

I also believe that what you will enjoy most about OneNote is its fun factor. You can color your pages, apply ruled lines, and create drawings. There is a nice collection of highlighters and colored markers you will definitely want to try out as well. So, now that you have a pretty, good understanding as to what OneNote is all about; it is time to get started.

Happy Computing!

Advisory:
Please be advised that Chapter 6 includes an overview of the OneNote Options menu that is not included in Office in a Minute, the 2010 comprehensive edition.

Chapter 1

Monday, August 06, 2012

1:52 PM

Getting Started

- ***Start the OneNote Application***
- ***Identify OneNote Screen Elements***
- ***Add Content to a Notebook***
- ***Enter Basic Text into a Notebook***

The estimated time required to complete all of these tasks is 6.5 minutes.

Getting Started

Launch the OneNote Application

The first thing we will need to do is to launch the OneNote application by locating its icon. To do this, you will want to perform the steps listed below.

1. Click on the Start button located at the lower left hand side of your desktop.
2. Locate the Microsoft OneNote icon and double-click your left mouse button.
3. Choose the New menu option.
4. Select My Computer.
5. Click into the Name field and type a name for your notebook.
6. Click on the Create Notebook button.

Figure 1

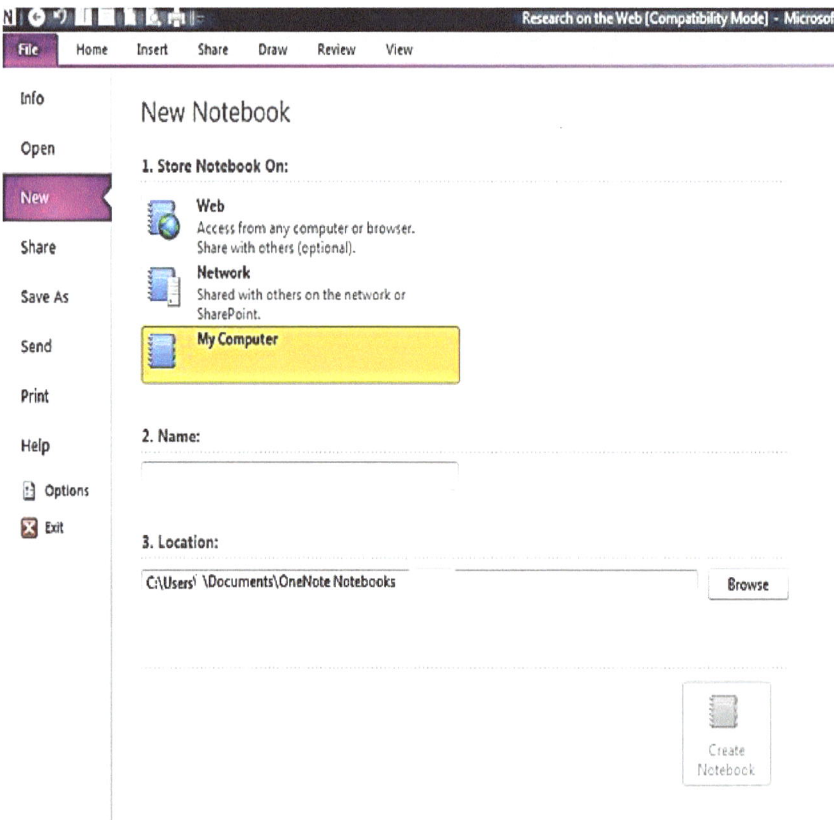

The OneNote Environment

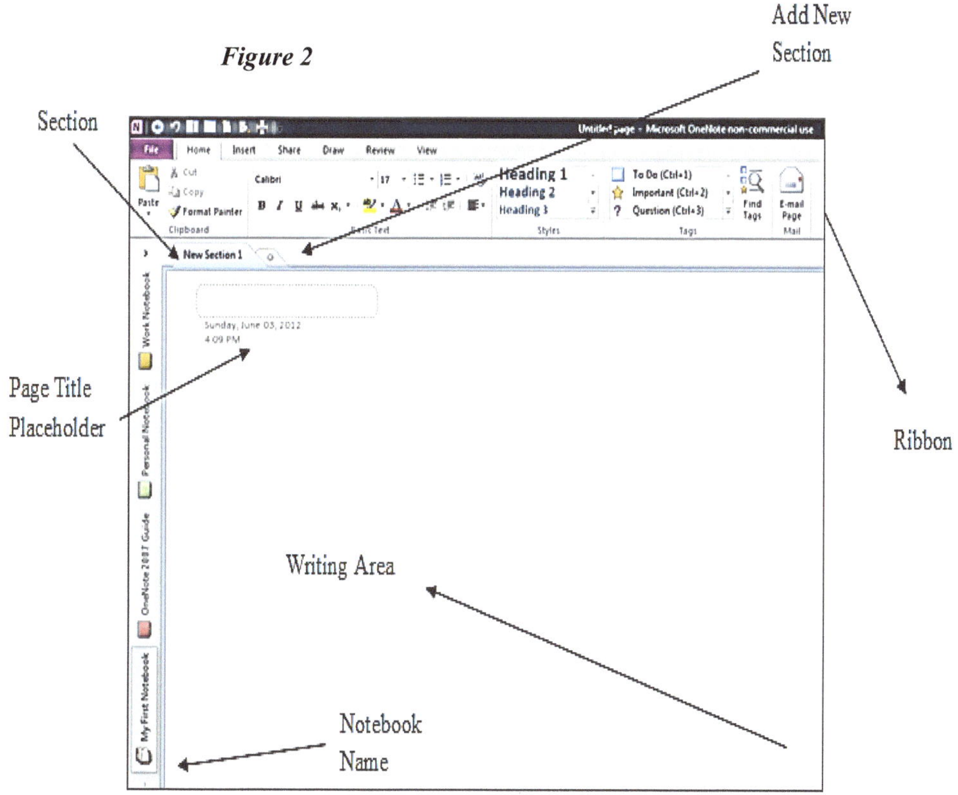

Figure 2

Ribbons, and Tabs, and Groups Oh My!

When OneNote opens beneath the title bar, you will see seven tabs with an activated Home ribbon. Each ribbon is divided into groups. For example, examine the groups that appear on Home ribbon, such as Clipboard, Basic Text, Styles, and Tags.

Section/Dividers

Like an actual loose-leaf binder, sections are designed to keep you organized. Microsoft's OneNote allows you to add as many additional sections as you need. Just below the ribbon is the section area. You can create as many notebooks, as you want; and, when you open a brand new notebook, one section tab appears along with an Add New Section tab button. A little later, you will learn how to add pages and sections to your first notebook.

Adding Content to a Notebook

One of the first things you will want to do is to enter a title for the first page of your new notebook. See Figure 3. Try typing a title within the Page Title Placeholder. After you type your title, notice that the title bar changes. Your notebook is automatically saved under the title you entered.

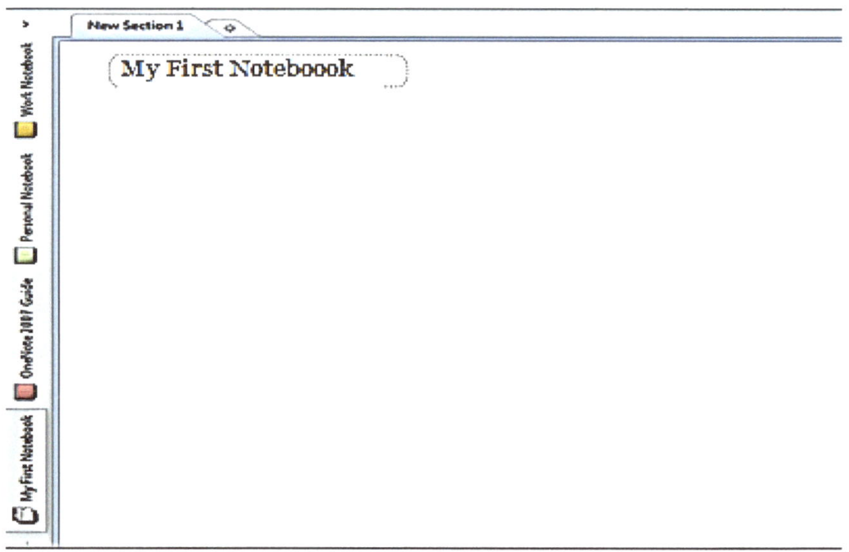

Figure 3

Entering Basic Text

If you click your mouse anywhere within the notebook area, a text window will open, and you will see your cursor flashing. Now you can begin entering basic text into your notebook.

Figure 4

Make Pretty Pages

OneNote Page with Rule Lines and "*Fireworks*" Page Template

Figure 5

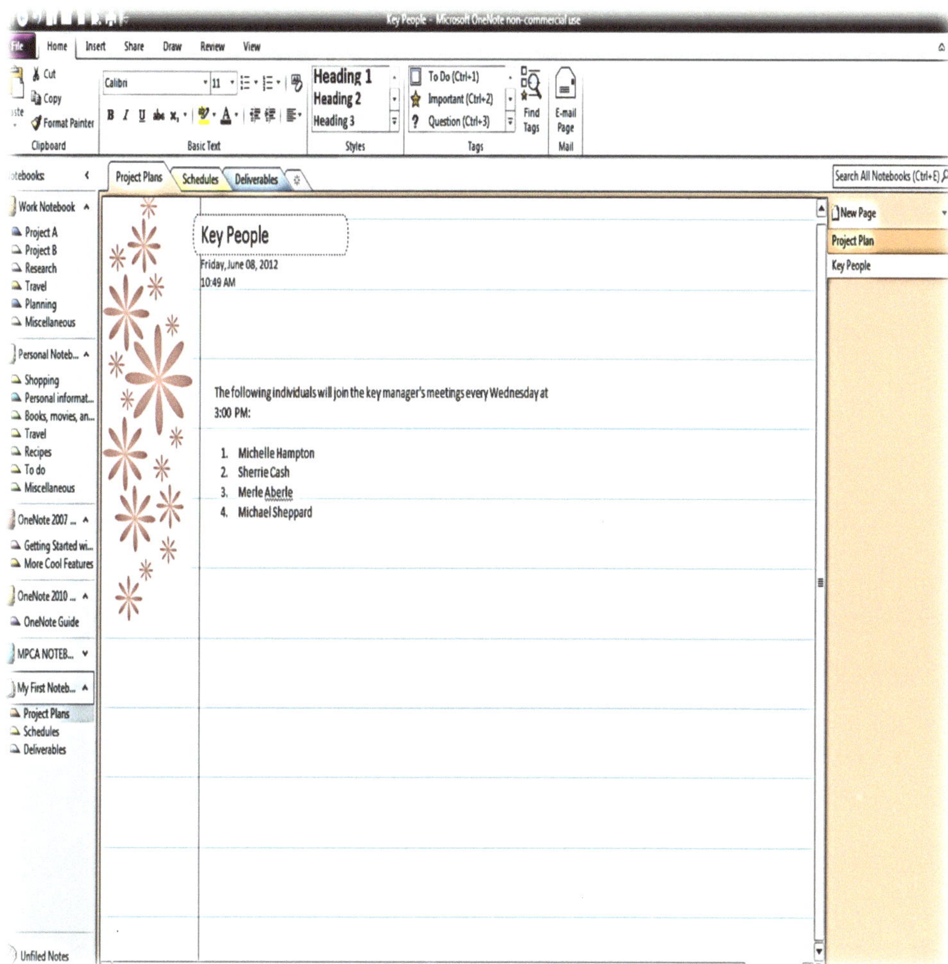

If you are interested adding an artistic element to your notebook, check out the wide variety of page templates that come bundled with Microsoft OneNote. You can change your page template at any time. We will discuss page templates in more detail in Chapter 2.

My Notes:

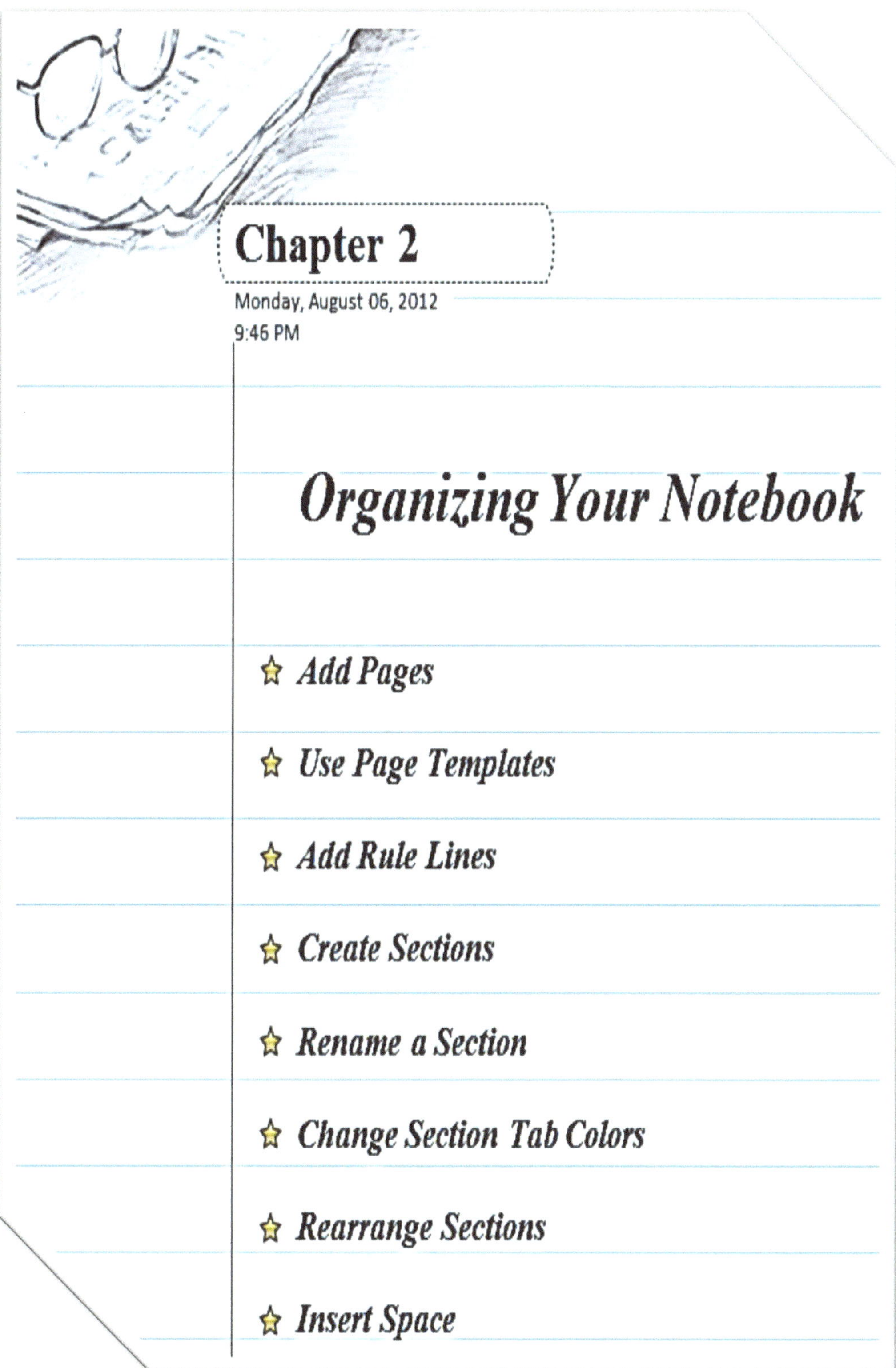

Chapter 2
Monday, August 06, 2012
9:46 PM
Organizing Your Notebook
Add Pages
Use Page Templates
Add Rule Lines
Create Sections
Rename a Section
Change Section Tab Colors
Rearrange Sections
Insert Space

The estimated time required to complete all of these tasks is 8 minutes.

Adding Pages to a Notebook

In about five seconds, you can add additional pages to your OneNote notebook just as you would add pages to a loose-leaf binder. To add a new page to your notebook

1. Click on the New Page button.
2. Type a title for your new page.

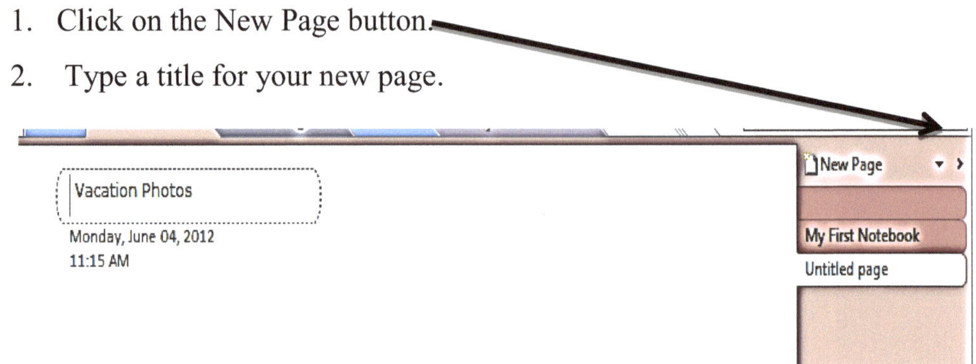

Figure 6

Page Templates

You can spice-up your notebook with a page template. When you click on the New Page drop down box (See Figure 6), several templates will appear on the menu. What is nice about this feature is that the template details will appear when the page is printed.

1. Click on the New Page drop-down list.
2. Choose the desired page design.

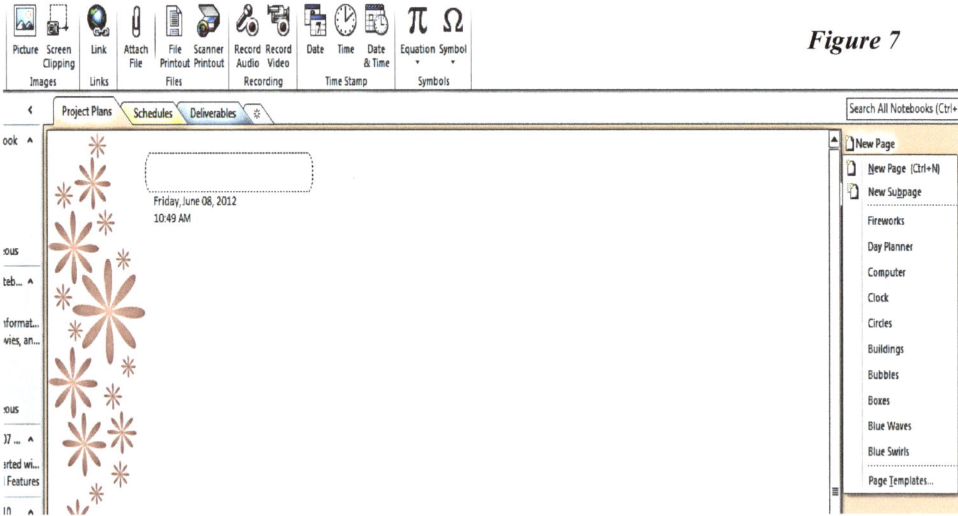

Figure 7

Downloading Notebook Templates from the Web

If you are looking for a kind of prefabricated notebook, take a look at the Templates on Office.com. Through OneNote, you can access a variety of notebook templates. Simply click on the Templates on Office.com link located in the Templates navigation pane. Your Web browser will open to the Microsoft Office Templates page. Choose the desired notebook template and then click on the download link. An Unpack Notebook dialog box like the one depicted in Figure 8 will appear. After you identify the template you want, choose the Create button.

Figure 8

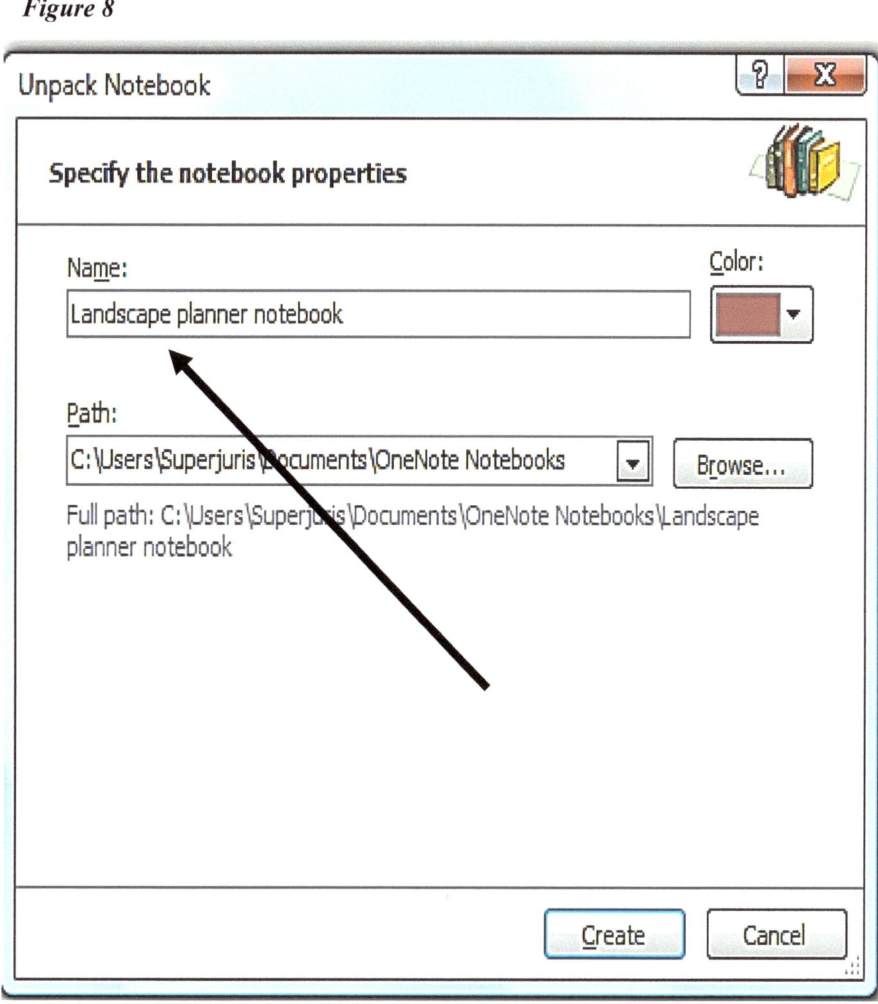

Change the Color of a Notebook Page

Add color to the pages of your notebook by selecting the View Tag. There you will find the Page Color button located within the Page Setup group. When you click on this button, OneNote will display a 16 pastel color pallet. See Figure 9 below. Note that page colors will appear only on screen, but will not print to a color-printer.

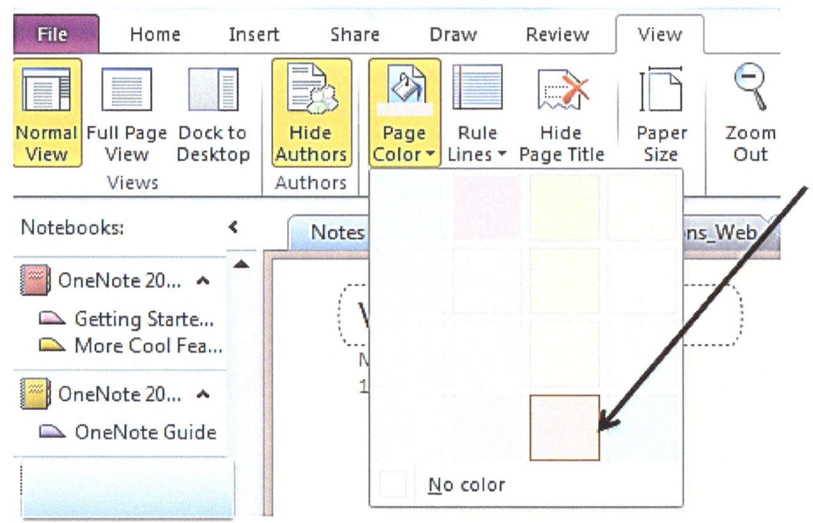

Figure 9

Add Rule lines to a Notebook Page

If you want to recreate the whole notebook look and feel, then you will appreciate OneNote's Rule Lines feature. You can choose from a variety of line styles by clicking on the Rule Lines drop-down list. See Figure 10.

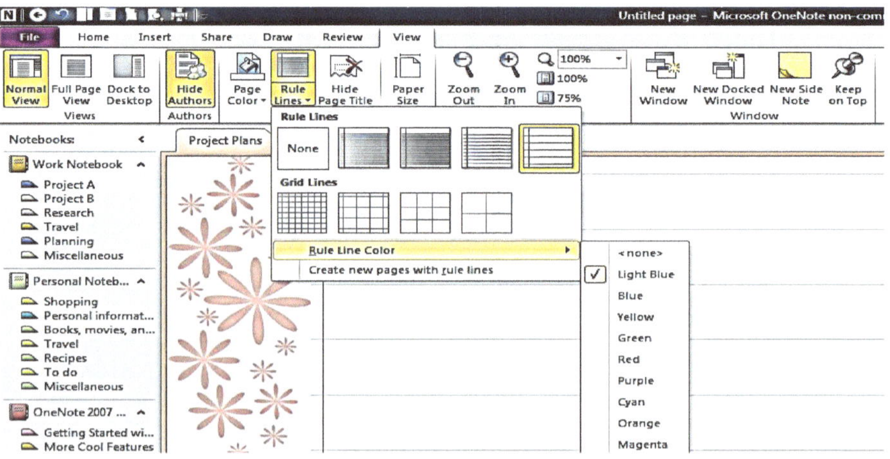

Figure 10

Get Organized by Creating Sections

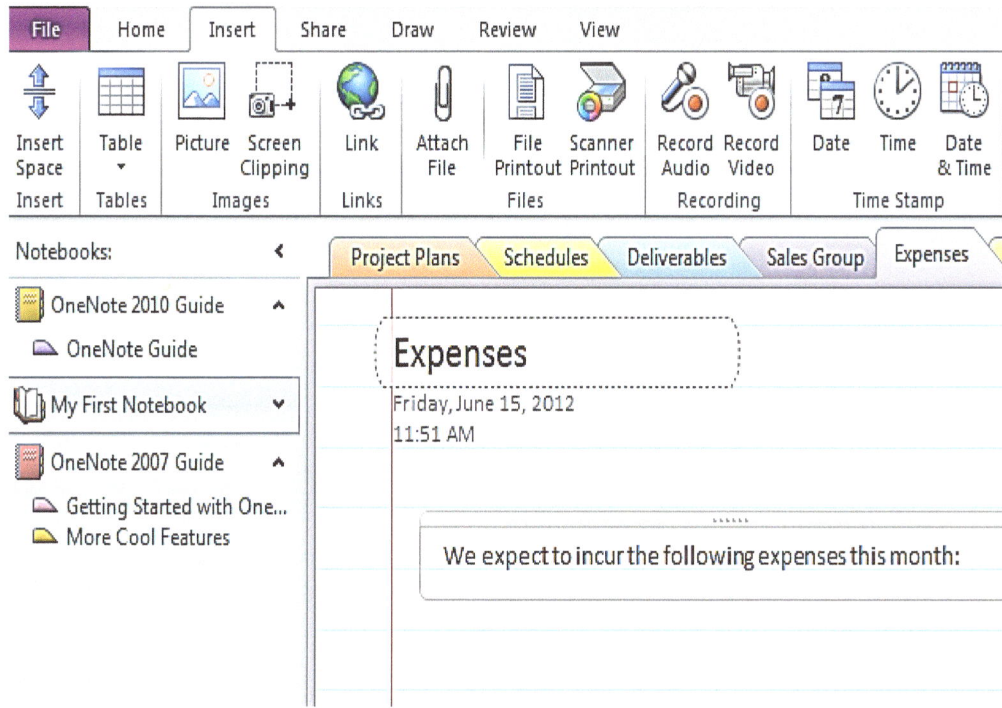

Figure 11

Creating sections within your notebook will help you organize your information. See Figure 11, and observe that we have created four sections: Project Plans, Schedules, Deliverables and Expenses.

As you will see on the following pages, OneNote makes the addition of sections very quick and easy to do. In seconds, you can create as many sections as you might need for your notebook. In addition, you can color your section tabs, rename and rearrange sections within your notebook.

Add Sections to a Notebook

Sections allow you to organize your notebook, and has been mentioned, you can create them very quickly. Before you do however, look at the OneNote window in Figure 12 and examine Section 1. OneNote automatically opens with one section each time a new notebook is created. Adjacent to the Section 1 tab is the New Section button. Clicking on this tab will place a new section tab within your notebook.

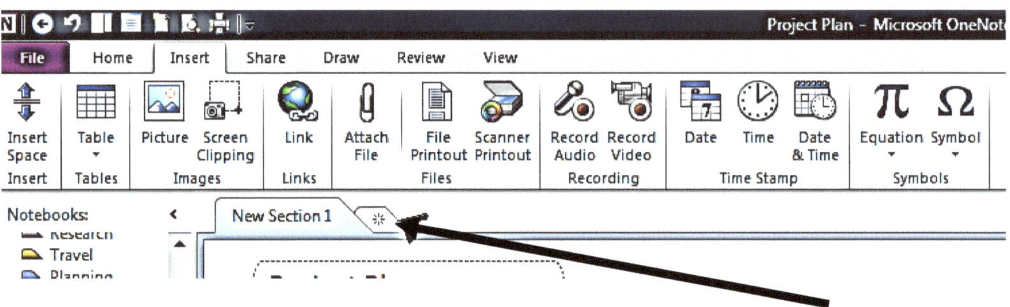

Rename a Section Tab

1. Point to the section tab you want to rename, and right click your mouse button.
2. Choose Rename.
3. Type the new section name.
4. Press the enter key.

Figure 12

Change Section Tab Colors

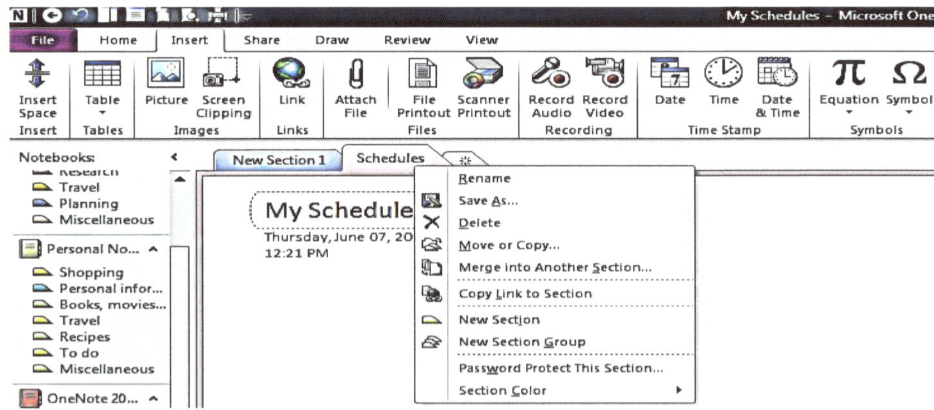

Figure 13

1. Point to the section tab you want to recolor and right click your mouse button.
2. Choose the Section Color option.
3. Choose the desired section color, and then press the enter key.

Rearrange Sections

With OneNote, you have the ability to rearrange your notebook pages and sections. See Figure 14. Assume that you want the Deliverables tab to become the second tab in our notebook.

1. Point and click on the section you wish to move.
2. Keep your finger on your left mouse button and drag your mouse to the desired location. (You will see what looks like a tiny square or document.)
   This is the section.
3. With your finger on your left mouse button, drag your mouse to drop the new section into the desired location.

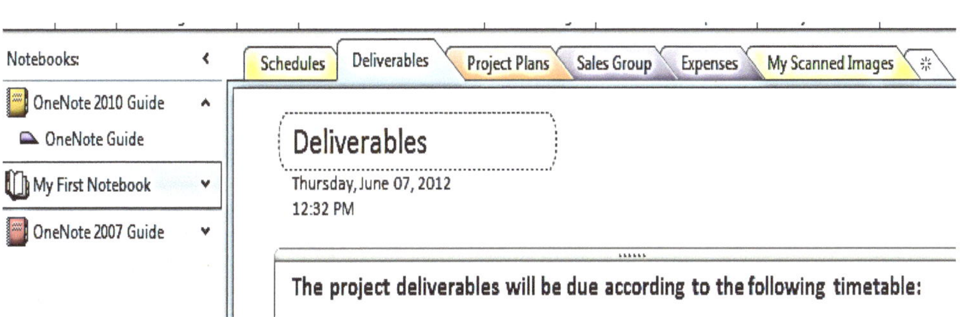

Figure 14

The Insert Space Feature

If you find yourself running out of space, you will adore OneNote's Insert Space feature. In less than sixty-seconds, you can increase the writing area within in your notebook.

To Add More Space to Your Notebook

1. Click on the Insert tab.
2. Click on the Insert Space button.
3. Move your mouse to the area where you want to insert more space. (A guide will appear.)
4. Click your left mouse button.

My Notes:

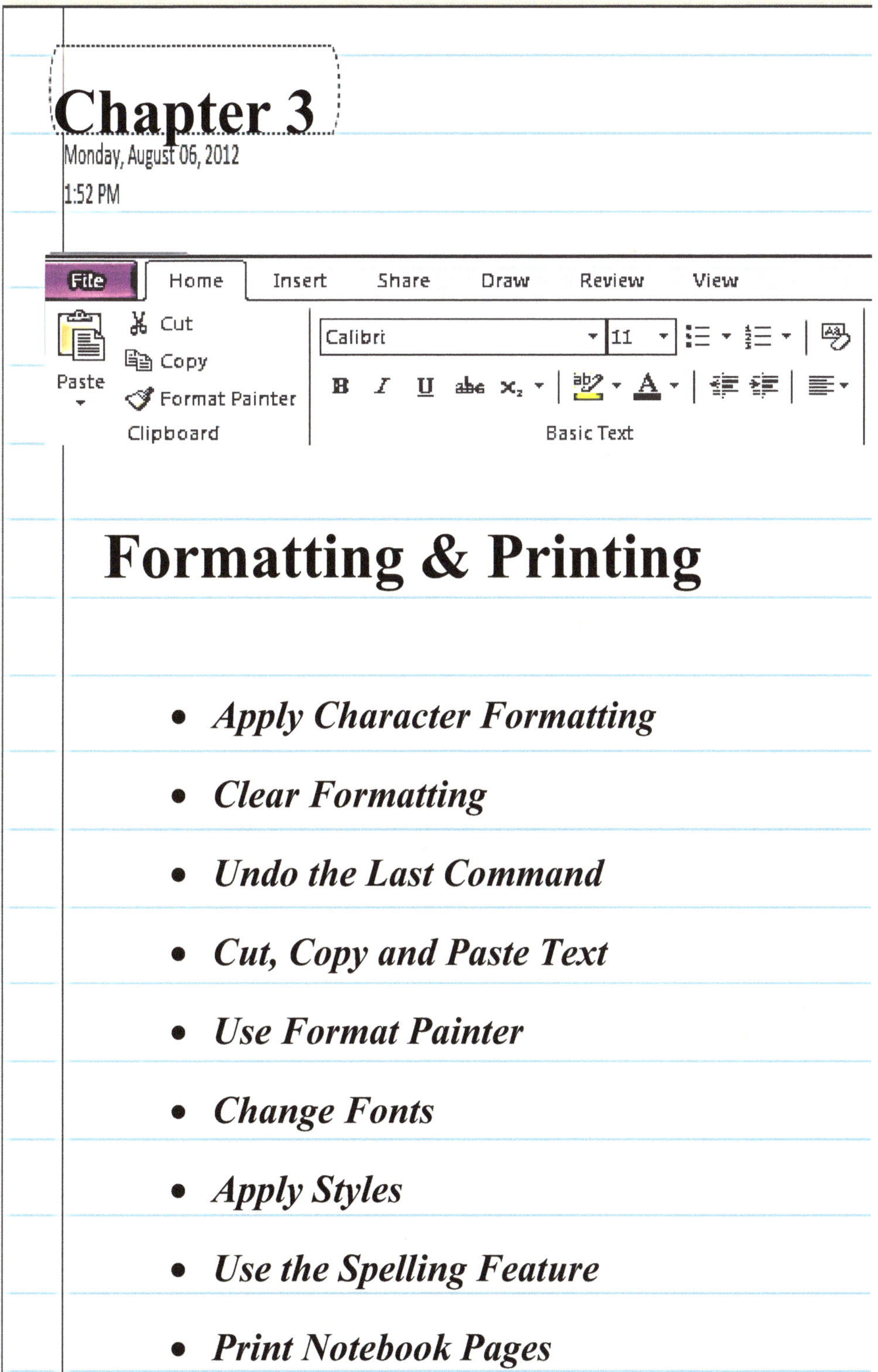

The estimated time required to complete all of these tasks is 10 minutes.

Character Formatting

You can focus your reader's attention by applying character formatting. With one keystroke and in less than five seconds, you can apply **bold**, underline, *italics*, or **color** to your text. Additionally, you can change the typeface of selected text just as you can in Microsoft Word. You will find these tools residing within the Basic Text group, which is located on the Home tab.

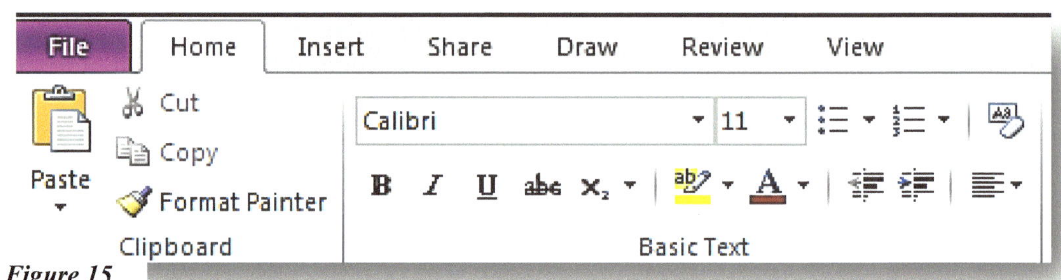

Figure 15

To Apply Character Formatting

1. Select the desired word, and then click on the [B] **Bold** button. Apply underline and *italics* formatting in the same way.

Clear Formatting

If you change your mind about text you have already formatted, simply do the following:

1. Select the desired text.
2. Click on the Clear Formatting button.

This will erase any formatting such as **bold**, underline, or *italics* from the selected text.

Undo the Last Command

You can undo your last keystrokes by clicking the Undo button. Think of this button as a do -over button. You will find this button located on the Quick Access Toolbar. Use it once and you will be hooked.

Using the Cut, Copy and Paste Feature

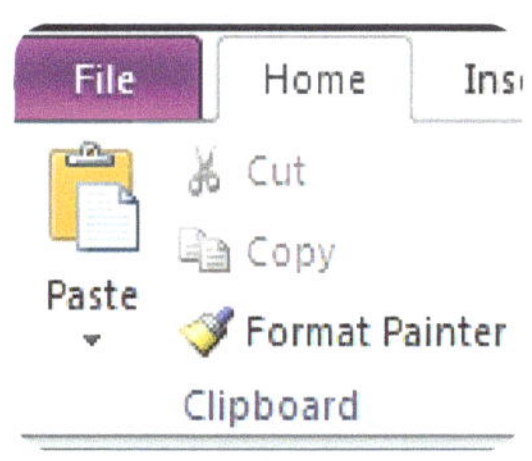

You may want to copy text from one location in your notebook to another. Alternatively, you can permanently move text to another section of your notebook. OneNote has a cut, copy and paste feature that allows you to do this in mere seconds.

Copied text is temporarily moved to the Clipboard. Think of the Clipboard as that magical place where data temporarily waits until you decide where to place it. There are several ways to copy and/or move text in OneNote. For example, if you want to copy text do the following:

1. Select the text you want to copy.
2. Click on the Home tab.
3. Click on the Copy button.
4. Place your mouse where you want the copied text to appear.
5. Click on the Paste button

Alternatively, you can highlight the selected text, and then use the short-cut keystroke, Ctrl + C to copy. Press Ctrl + V to paste the text where you it to appear.

To Remove or Cut Text

1. Select the text you want to cut.
2. Click on the Cut (scissor icon).

Save Time with Format Painter

If you have worked with Microsoft Word, then you already know what a time-saver the Format Painter can be. This feature allows you to copy the character formatting of a word and then apply it to another word, sentence or paragraph.

To Use Format Painter

1. Click on the Home tab.
2. Select the word that contains the desired formatting.
3. Click on the Format Painter to copy the formatting.
4. Select the text to be formatted.

Apply a New Font

To Change From the Arial to the Times New Roman Font

1. Select the text to be formatted.
2. Click on the Font drop down box and choose the desired font.
3. Click on the Font Size button if you also wish to change the size of the text.

Figure 16

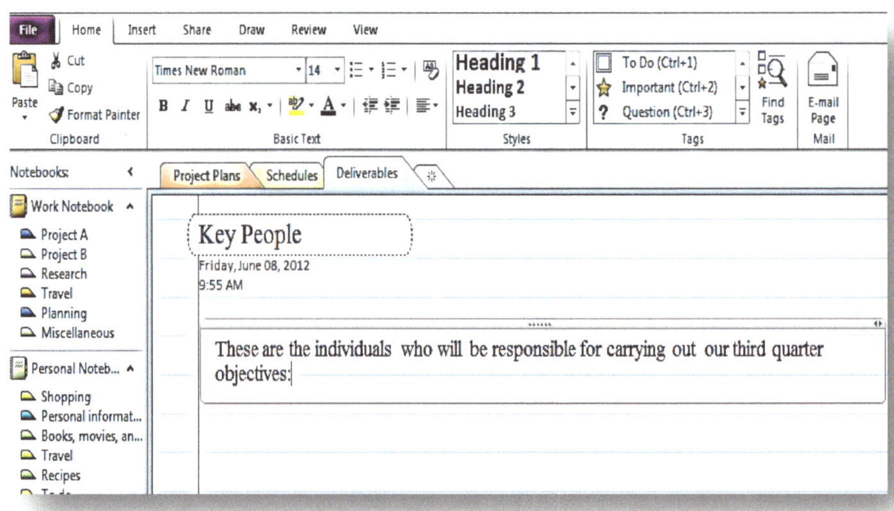

Apply Styles to Basic Text and Save Time

If you are interested in saving some time on formatting your text, consider using the Styles feature. Anyone who has worked with Microsoft Word is likely to be familiar with how to use styles, but if you are a novice, take heart. Think of styles as a kind of preformatting. For example, look at the Styles group located on the Home tab. See Figure 16. The style **Heading 1** is made up of the **Calibri** Font is **bold** and has a 17-point font size. Using Styles can save you the steps it normally takes to select a font, a character format and font size.

To Apply a Heading Style

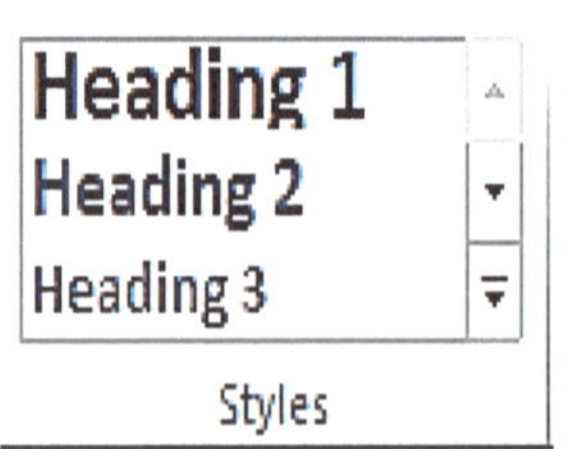

1. Click on the Home tab.
2. Select the desired text.
3. Click on the desired heading style.

Spell Checking with OneNote

Microsoft OneNote contains a spelling feature that will automatically check your document for common spelling errors. In addition, you can quickly spell check a word by selecting it, and then clicking on the Spelling button. Be advised that proper nouns and words typed in all capitals are generally **not** reviewed by the Spelling feature.

1. Click on the OneNote Review tab, and then click on the Spelling button.
2. To accept a suggested correction, click the Change button.

If unique words appear in your notebook that you do not wish to have the Spelling program flag, click on the Add to Dictionary button.

Figure 17

If you are familiar with the spelling and grammar feature in Microsoft's Word, Excel and PowerPoint applications, be advised that OneNote does not include a grammar-checking program. Unlike in Word and Excel, you will also not find a Thesaurus.

Researching with OneNote

Research is a OneNote feature that you will really come to appreciate. While you are working within your notebook, you can access references such as dictionaries, encyclopedias and translation services without leaving the OneNote environment. When you click on the Research button, a pane opens up on the right side of the screen. See Figure 18 below. Notice that a number of different online resources can be searched.

To use the Research Feature

1. Click on the Review tab.
2. Type a subject into the Search for field.
3. Press the enter key [→].

Figure 18

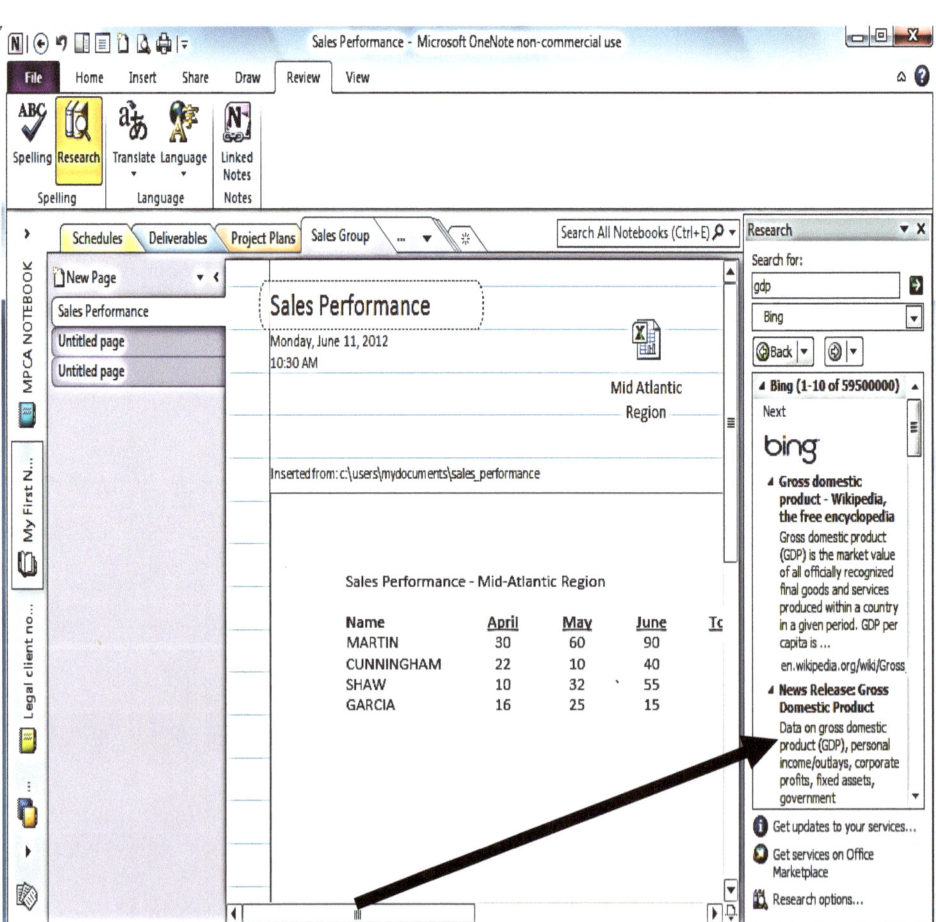

Printing Notebook Pages

If you have worked with other applications such as Word or Excel, you may find the print option in OneNote, a bit unfamiliar. Keep in mind that when you choose the Print option from the File tab, all of your existing notebooks will appear on the backstage menu. You must first select the notebook you wish to print, and then choose Print Preview.

When the Print Preview and Settings dialog box opens, you will have the opportunity to select the print range, letter size and orientation. Examine the Print Preview window in Figure 19. From this dialog box, you can choose to place footer in your printed notebook page.

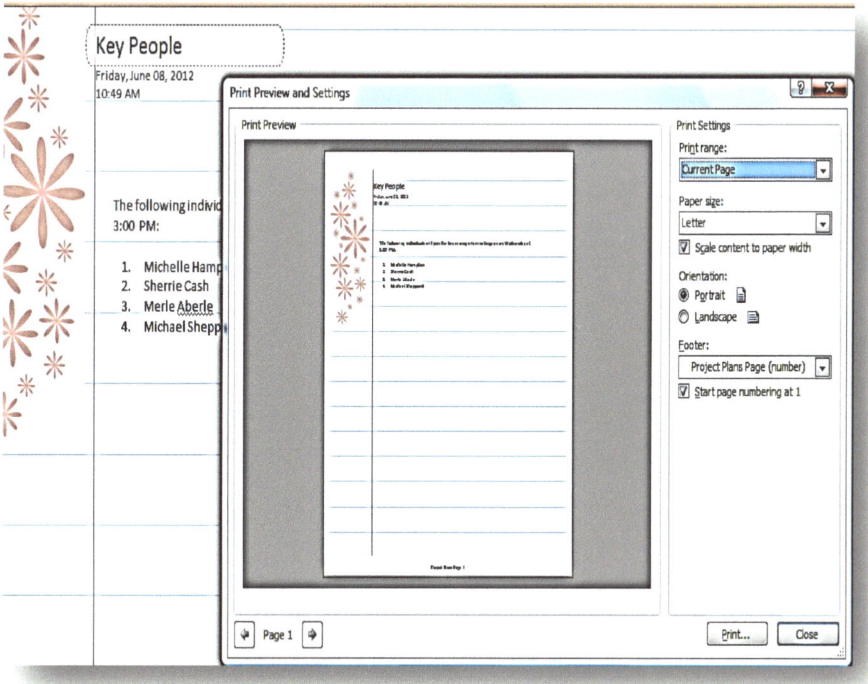

Figure 19

To Print in OneNote

1. Click on the File tab.
2. Click on the Notebook you wish to print.
3. Choose the Print Preview button.
4. Select the print range.
5. Click on the Print button.

My Notes:

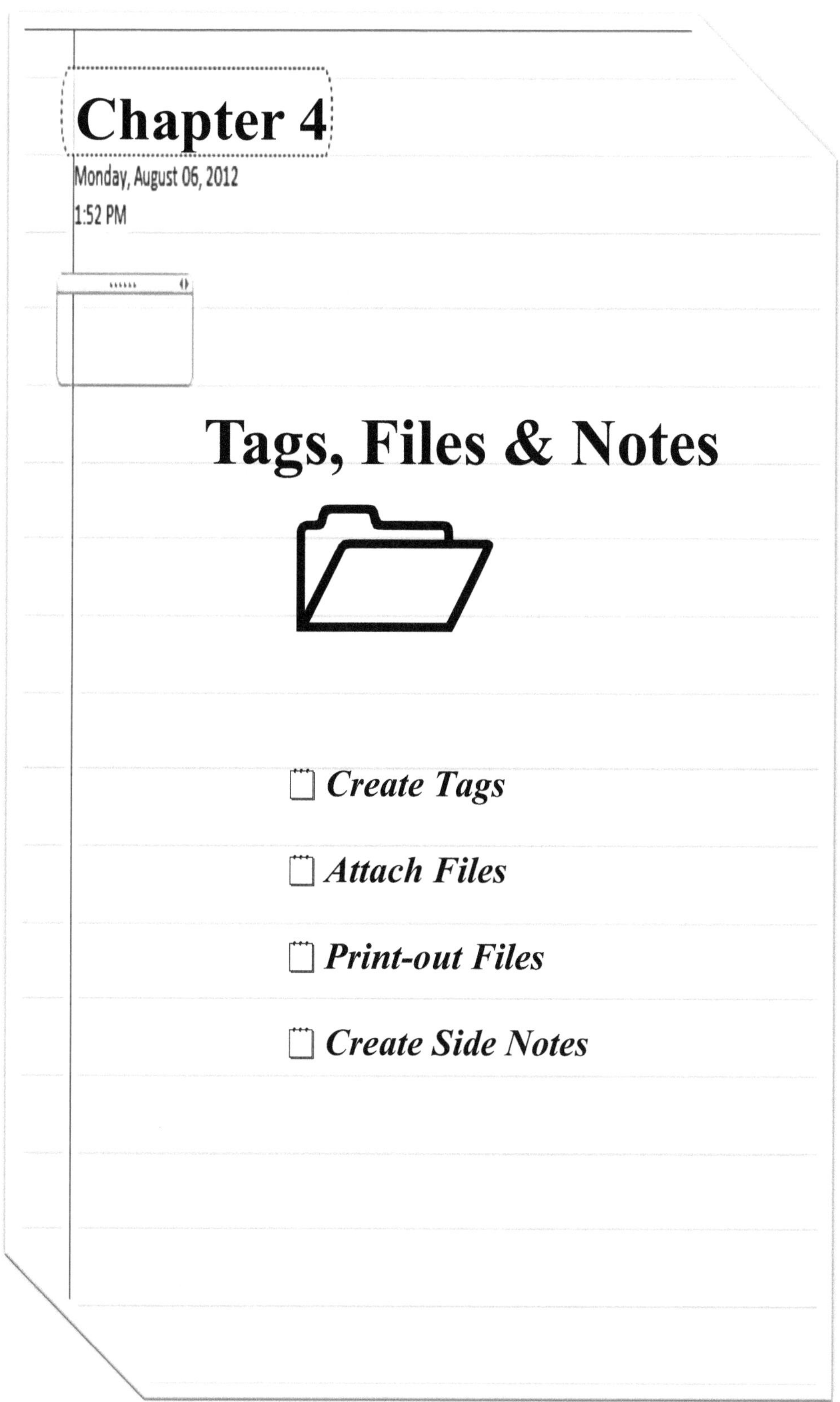

Chapter 4
Monday, August 06, 2012
1:52 PM
Tags, Files & Notes
Create Tags
Attach Files
Print-out Files
Create Side Notes

The estimated time required to complete all of these tasks is 5.5 minutes.

Tags for Task Management

Figure 20

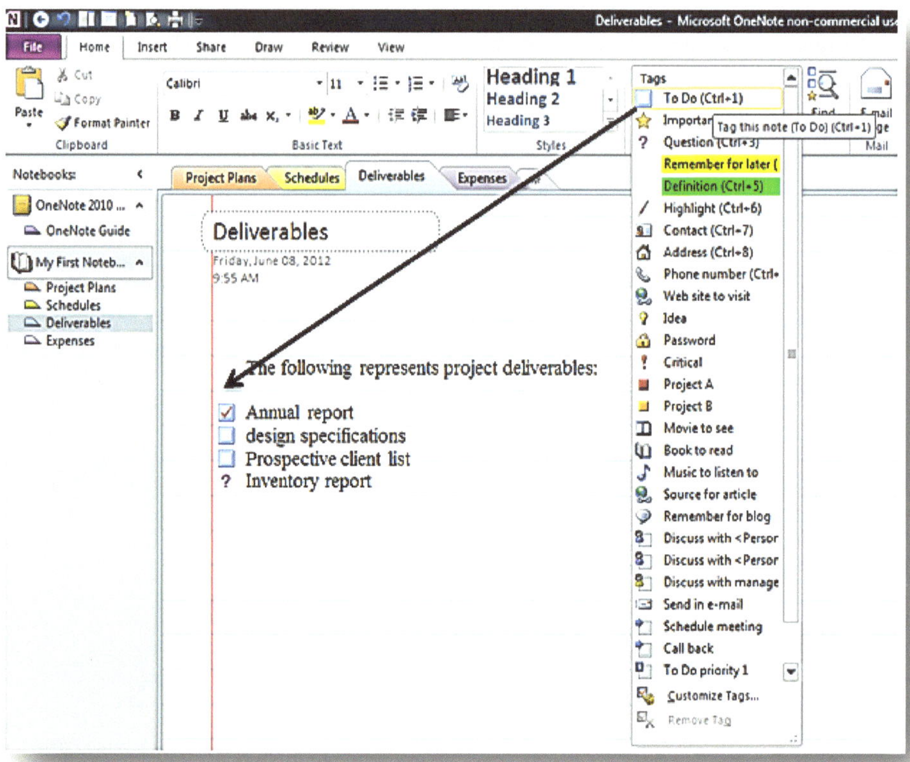

Organization is one of the cornerstones of the OneNote application. OneNote's Tags feature enables you to mark, prioritize, and categorize tasks by tagging your notes. See Figure 20. Notice the tags adjacent to the "Prepare annual report" item. You can quickly mark items as Important or place question tags in your notebook text. In fact, there are more than 20 different tags available. In addition, OneNote also enables you to create your own customized tags.

To Insert a Tag

1. Click on the Home tab.
2. Place your cursor where you want the tag to appear.
3. Click on the Tags Group drop-down list.
4. Choose the desired tag.

Note: To remove a tag, point to the tag, right click your mouse button and select Remove Tag.

Attaching Files to Notebook Pages

One of the coolest features within OneNote is Attach File. This feature enables you to place a copy of a file located on your computer (document, music, etc.,) within any one of your notebook pages.

Figure 21

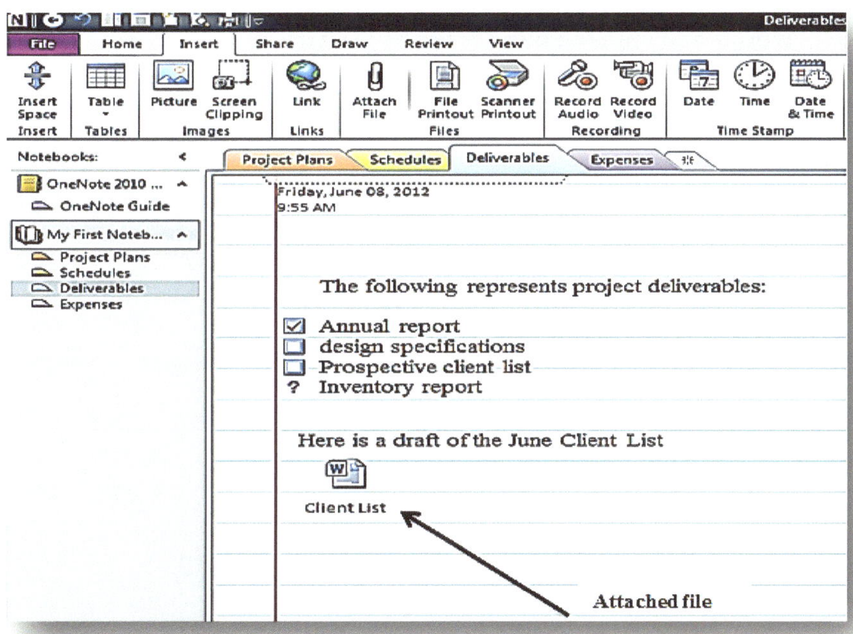

To Attach a File to a Notebook Page

1. Click on the Insert tab.
2. Place your cursor where you want the attached file to appear.
3. Click on the Attach File button.
4. Locate the desired file.
5. Click on the Insert button.

To Use the File Printout Feature

1. Click on the Insert tab.
2. Place your cursor where you want the printed file to appear.
3. Click on the File Printout button.
4. Locate the desired file.
5. Click on the Insert button.

Printing Text from External Applications

If you have information stored in other applications, such as Microsoft Word, Excel, PowerPoint or Access, you will be pleased to learn that you can save and print that information to your notebook. For example, assume you wish to include and place a workbook you created in Microsoft Excel within a notebook page. If you choose the Printer drop-down list, from within the Excel application, a list of printers appears. Notice that one print option is to print the document to OneNote 2010. See Figure 22.

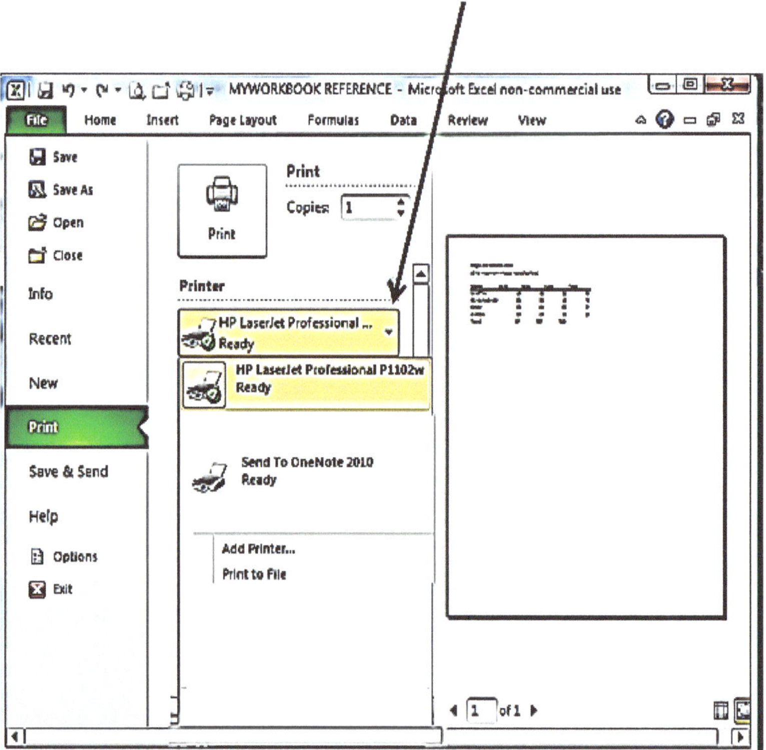

Figure 22

To Send an External File to OneNote

1. Open the desired file.
2. Click on the File tab.
3. Choose the Print option.
4. Click on the Printer drop-down list, as though you are choosing another printer.
5. Select the Send to OneNote 2010 option. Continued on the next page☛

After you select the Print button, the Select Location in OneNote dialog box will open. The OneNote application will prompt you to identify where in your notebook(s) you want your text to appear. See Figure 23 below.

To Select a Location

1. Click into the Location field.
2. Select the page in which you want to place your document from All Notebooks.
3. Choose the OK button.

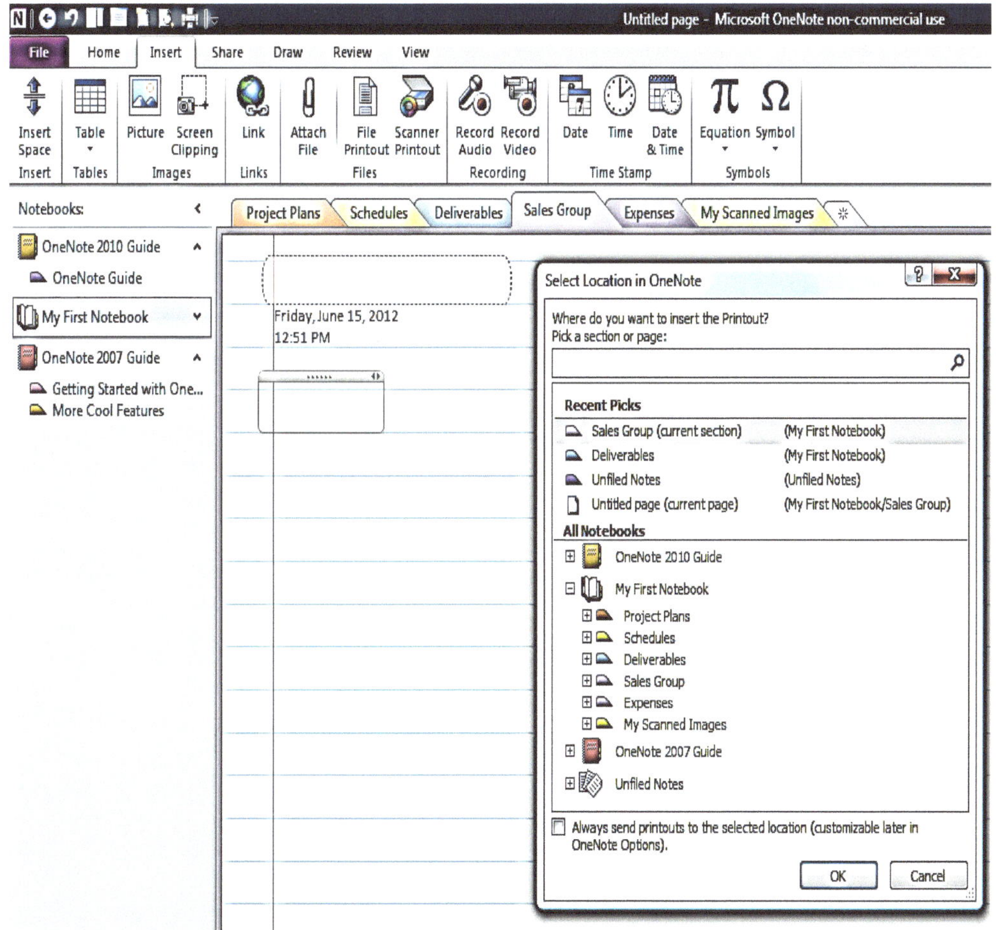

Figure 23

Bring Sticky Notes to Life with Side Note

If you have ever used those popular little sticky notes as temporary reminders, you will genuinely appreciate Side Note. This feature will enable you to create temporary notes that you can keep open on your desktop. See Figure 24.

Figure 24

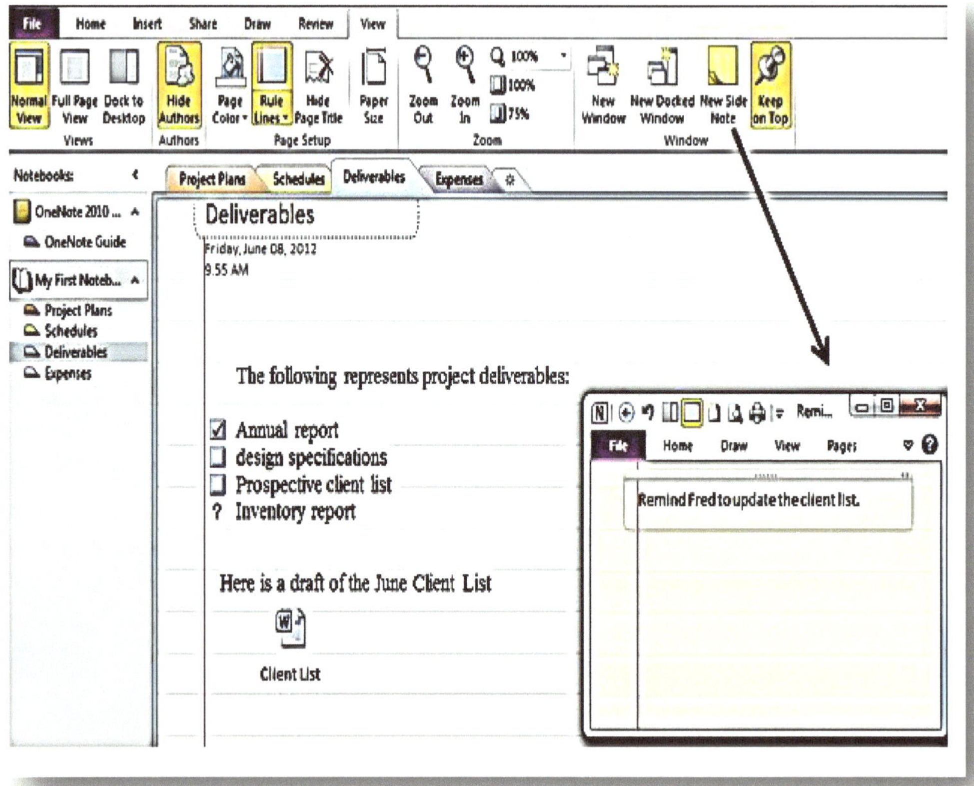

To Create a Side Note

1. Click on the View tab.
2. Place your cursor anywhere within your notebook.
3. Click on the New Side Note button located within the Window Group.
4. Type your note.

To anchor your side note, click on the Keep on Top button, also located within the Window group of the View ribbon.

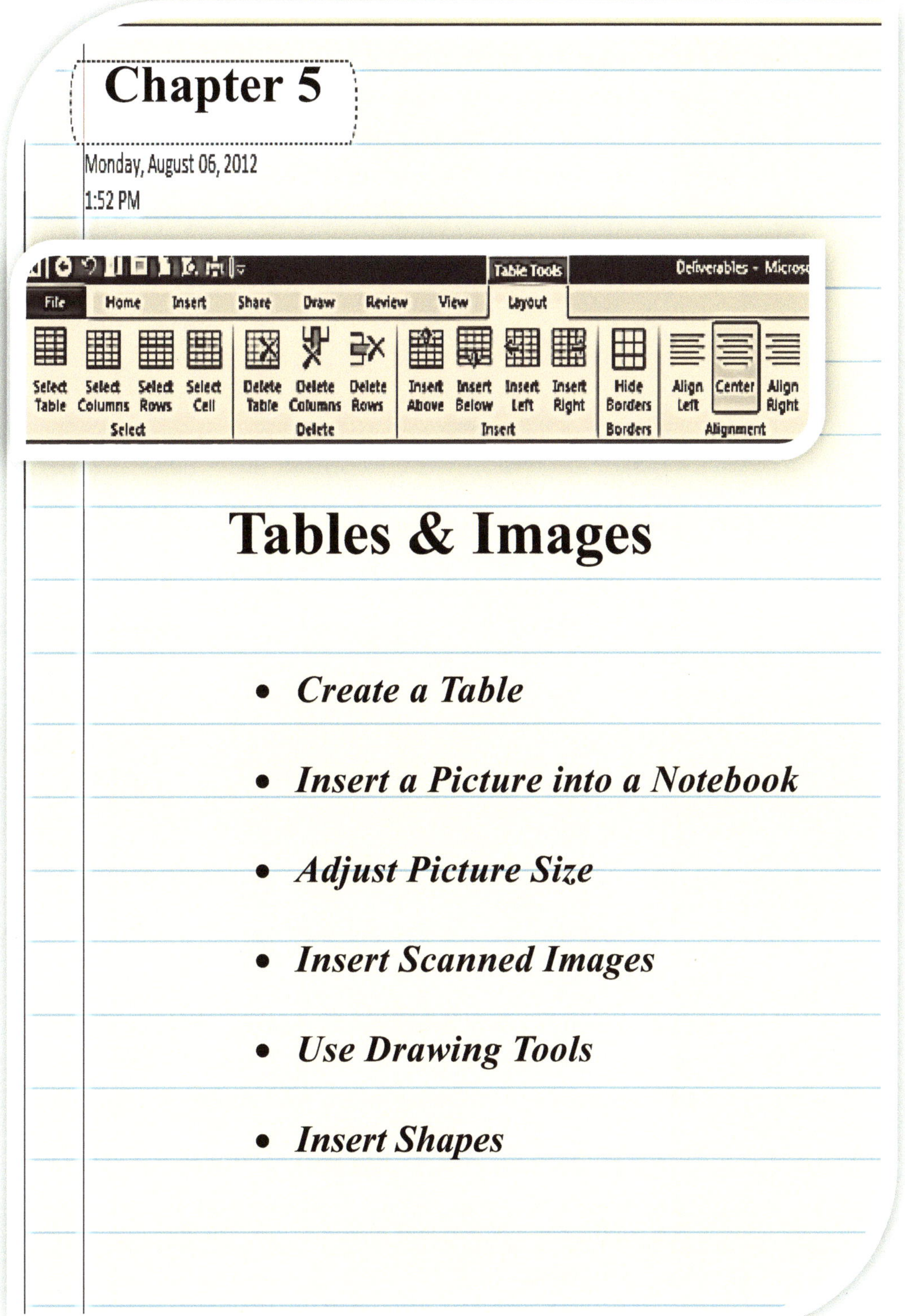

The estimated time required to complete all of these tasks is 16 minutes.

Creating Tables in OneNote

Tables can enhance your ability to organize text, and fortunately, they are very easy to create with OneNote. If you have worked with tables in Microsoft Word or PowerPoint, you will recognize OneNote's basic table functions. However, before you decide to skip this section, you should know that Tables in OneNote lack the elegance and full functionality available in Word. For example, there is no table design gallery in OneNote. The differences may take a little getting used to, but it is worth it to spend a little time reviewing the OneNote version.

Figure 25

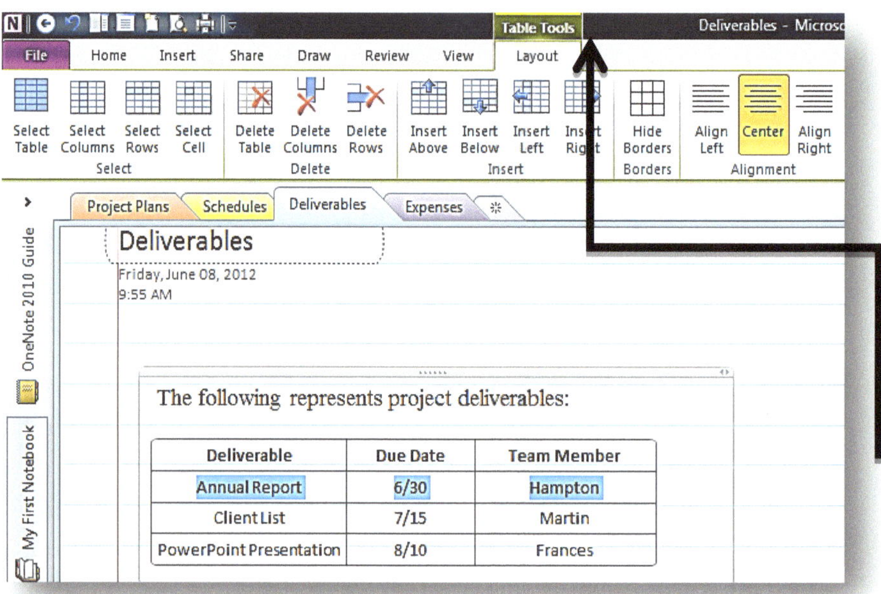

Familiar table options include Select Table, Insert Column and Row Above as well as text alignment buttons, such as Left, Center, Right and Justify. The Table Tools tab appears after you have inserted a table into your notebook. See Figure 25.

To Insert a Table into a Notebook Page

1. Click on the page where you want the table to appear.
2. Choose the View tab.
3. Click on the Insert Table button.
4. Choose the desired number of columns and rows.
5. Click on the OK button.

Inserting Picture into a Notebook Page

Pictures can be easily inserted into your notebook with OneNote's Insert Picture feature. When you click on the Insert Picture button, OneNote will enable you to select a picture from any location on your computer.

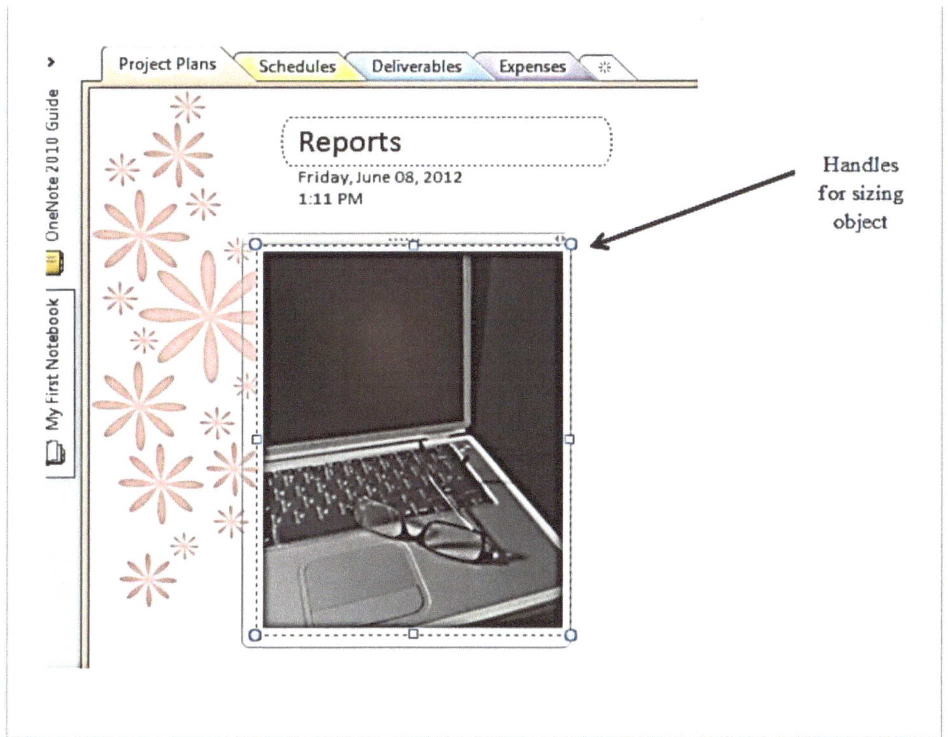

Figure 26

Adjust the Size of Your Picture

After you select your photograph or Clip Art, OneNote places it into your document surrounded by handles. See Figure 26.

To make an image larger or smaller, simply hover with your mouse over any of the handles, and notice the double arrow. When the double arrow appears, hold down your left mouse button to size the image.

Inserting and Managing Scanned Images

Another one of OneNote's best features is Scanner Printout. If you have paper documents that you want to preserve in digital form, you will find it relatively easy to scan them into your Notebook. When you click on the Scanner Printout button, OneNote will automatically communicate with your scanner and place the document into your Notebook. In the graphic below, we have scanned a page from Microsoft's OneNote Tutorial. Of course, to make this work you must have a scanner.

Figure 27

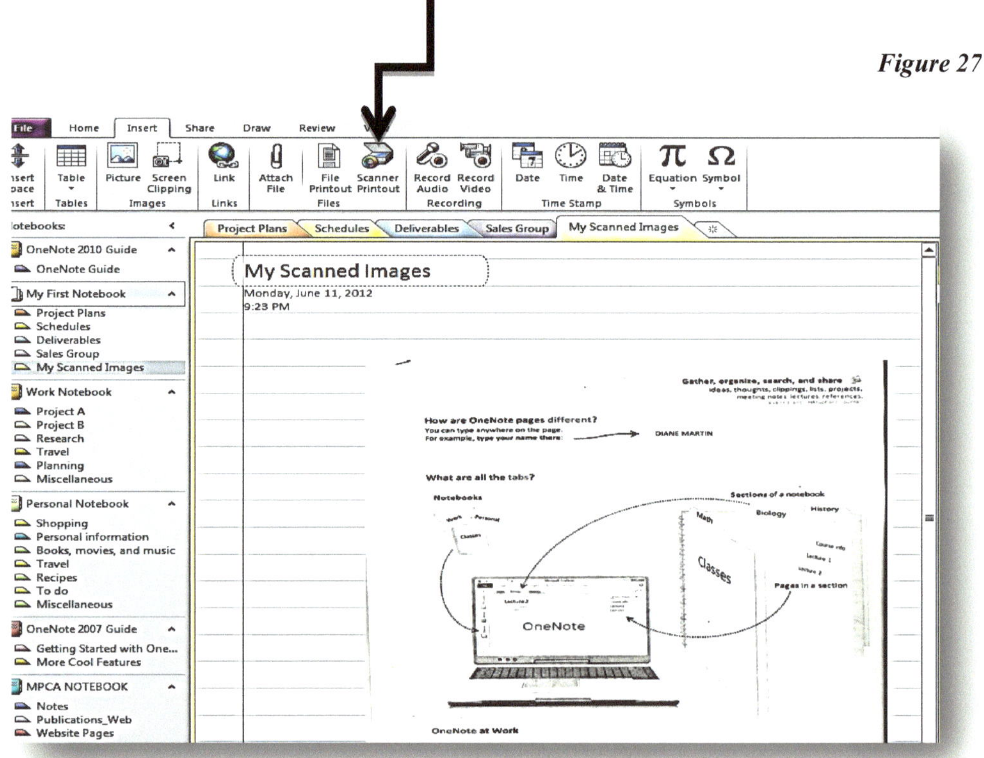

To Scan Documents into a Notebook

1. Place the document face down on your scanner
2. Click into the page where you want the scanned image to appear.
3. Select the Insert tab.
4. Click the Scanner Printout button.

Working with OneNote's Drawing Tools

Highlight or mark-up text within your notebook with OneNote's Drawing tools. Click on the Draw tab to view the Tools group. There are more than 30 marker size and/or color options from which to choose. For example, notice how we highlighted the June numbers displayed in Figure 28.

1. Click on the yellow highlighter button and drag your mouse across the desired text.
2. Press the Select & Type button to turn off highlighting.

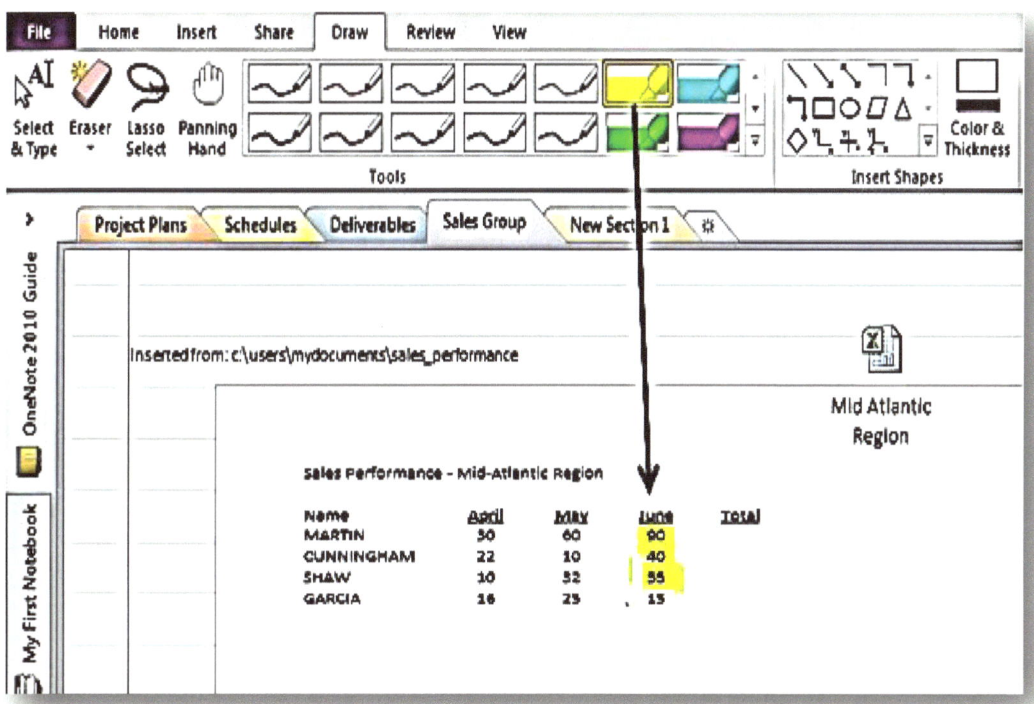

Figure 28

You can erase marked or highlighted text by using the Eraser tool located at the top left hand side of the Tools Group. See Figure 28.

1. Click on the Eraser tool.
2. Drag your mouse across the highlighted text.
3. Press the Select & Type button to turn off the Eraser.

OneNote Drawing Tools

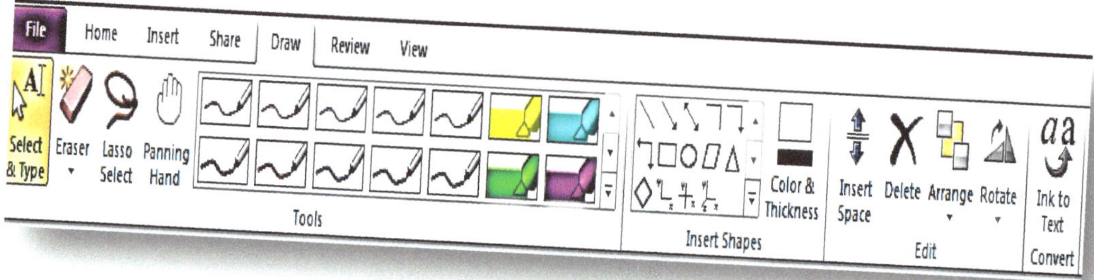

Select & Type:	Use this tool to select an object or type text.
Eraser:	Just like its namesake, this tool allows you to erase any marks you made with drawing tools.
Lasso Select:	This tool allows you to select any free form objects or text you created with marking tools. Once selected you can move, or modify the selected objects.
Panning Hand:	Use the Panning Hand to scroll through a page.
Tools:	The Tools group contains various markers and highlighters. Use these tools to either highlight text or create free-form objects.
Insert Shapes:	This group contains a variety of shapes that you can insert into a notebook page.
Color & Thickness:	This feature allows you to control the color and thickness of any objects you create.
Delete:	When chosen, it deletes any selected object whether text or graphic.
Arrange:	Use this feature to control the order or placement of more than one object on the page.
Ink to Text:	Use this tool to convert free from objects to typed text.

Shape Your Ideas

OneNote's Insert Shapes feature is still impressive though not as extensive as that found in Microsoft Word. With this feature, you can quickly insert basic shapes within your notebook and add color as well. You will find the Insert Shapes button located within the ribbon of the Draw tab. See Figure 29.

To Insert a Shape

1. Click on the Draw tab.
2. Select the page where you want to place the shape.
3. Click on the desired shape within the Insert Shapes group.
4. As soon as the cursor turns into a cross hair, draw the shape.

Figure 29

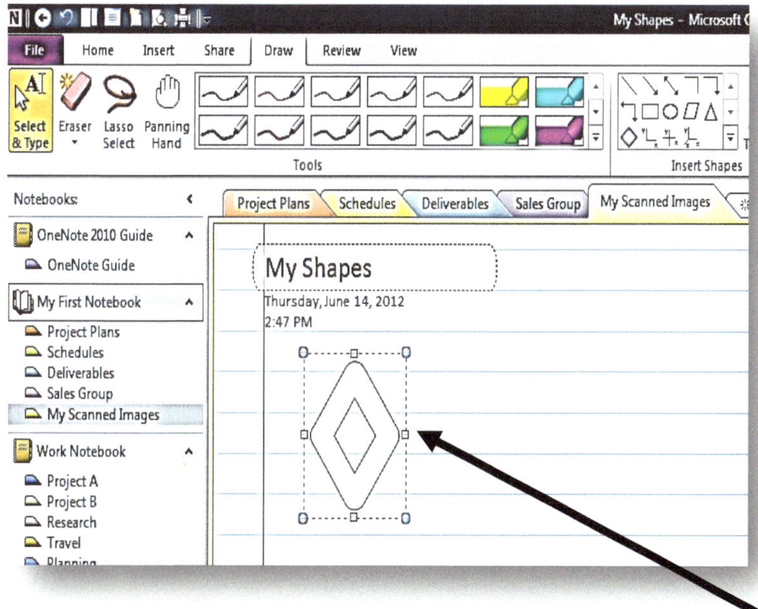

Notice in the graphic above that the shape has handles. Remember, this means that you can size the shape, making it larger or smaller.

To delete a shape, select it, and when the handles appear, press the delete key.

My Notes:

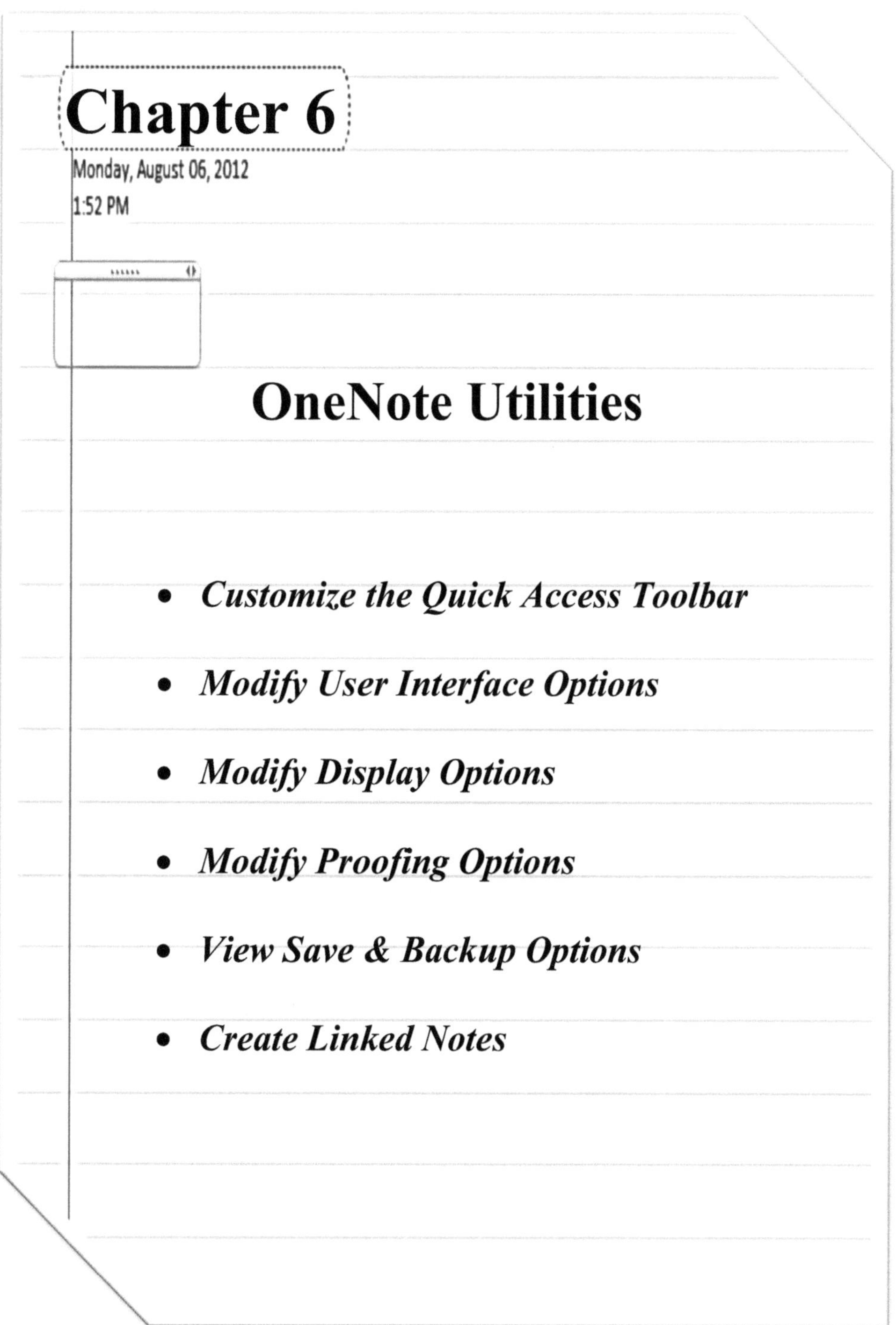

Chapter 6
Monday, August 06, 2012
1:52 PM
OneNote Utilities
Customize the Quick Access Toolbar
Modify User Interface Options
Modify Display Options
Modify Proofing Options
View Save & Backup Options
Create Linked Notes

The estimated time required to complete all of these tasks is 8.5 minutes

Customize the Quick Access Toolbar

Place frequently used commands where you can quickly access them, by customizing the Quick Access toolbar. You can find the Quick Access toolbar just below the ribbons.

To Customize the Quick Access Toolbar

1. Select the File menu.
2. Click on Options.
3. Choose Quick Access toolbar.
4. Choose the desired command from the Popular Commands drop-down list.
5. Click on the Add button>>.
6. Choose the OK button.

Figure 30

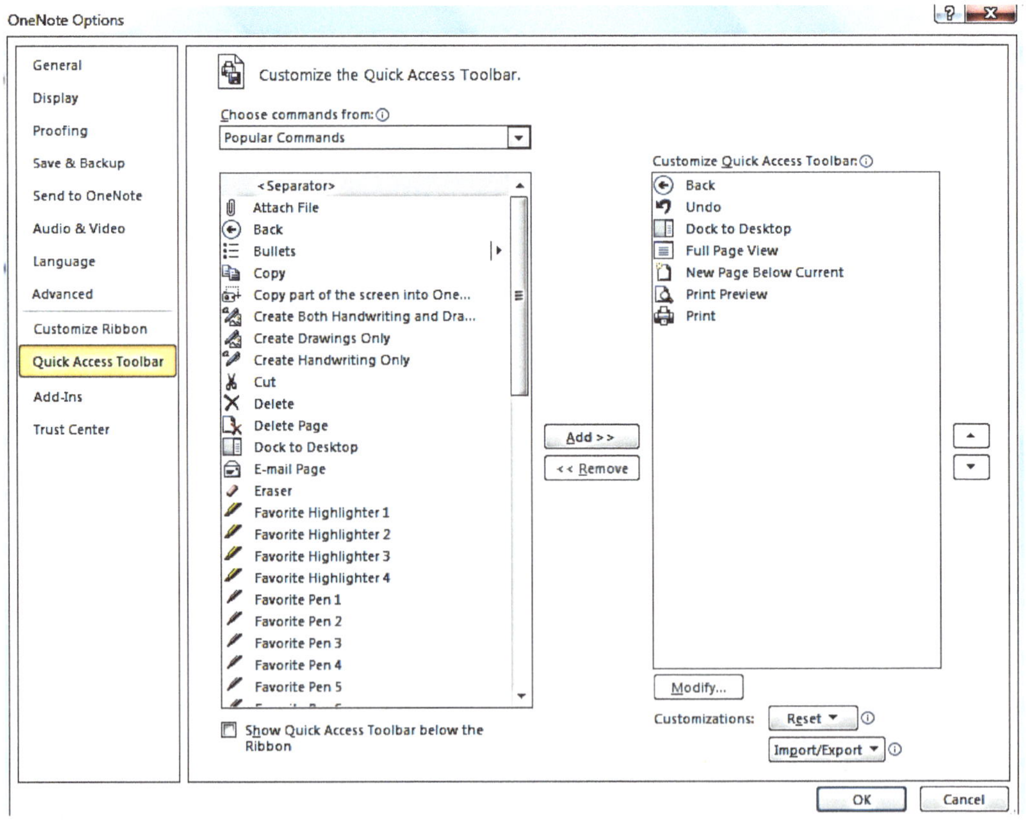

Change General Settings -- Options Dialog Box

OneNote like other Microsoft Office applications comes with certain default settings. For example, you may recall that the font is not something you initially chose. A default font is selected for you so you can begin typing as soon as you open the application. However, for a variety of reasons, you may prefer or actually require a different typeface. For this reason, you have the option of changing many of the default settings applicable to OneNote. To change default settings, you will once again be required to access the Options dialog box. See Figure 31.

Click on the File tab and choose Options. There are several tabs within this dialog box, and here we will begin a brief review of the types of changes you can make to the OneNote environment.

Figure 31

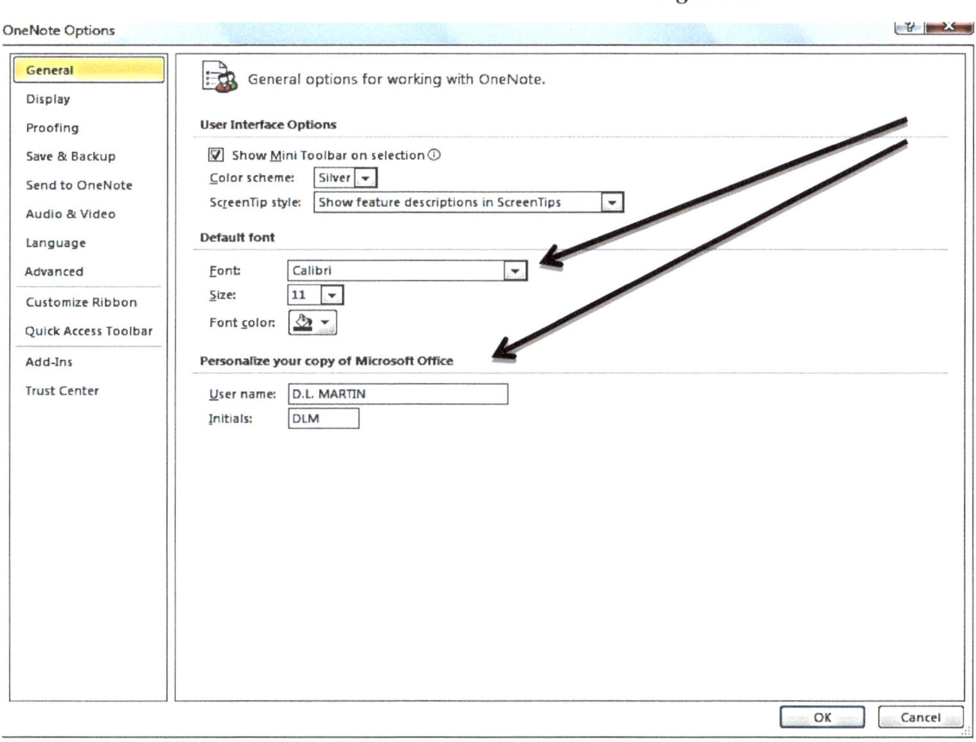

When you select Options from the File menu, observe that the General Options dialog box is presented first. Here you can perform a highly recommended task. First, notice the Default Font section. What you are observing in Figure 31 is Calibri as the default font. The font size is 11 points and the font color is black. Notice that each option here is accompanied by a drop-down list. Click on any of these drop-down listes to change the default setting and then choose OK. Each time you open OneNote; the new setting will apply and become your default setting.

Below the Default Font section is the Personalize your copy of Microsoft Office section. This is an opportunity to type both your initials and username.

Display Options

If you like the appearance of rule lines in your notebook, choose Display from the Options menu, and then click the Create all new pages with rule lines checkbox depicted in Figure 32. If you have already begun working with side notes, another very nice feature is the Dock new Side Note windows option. Selecting this feature ensures that your side notes will be anchored to the desktop whenever you open OneNote.

Change the location of your Page tabs from the right side of the screen to the left side by clicking into Page tabs appear on the left option.

Figure 32

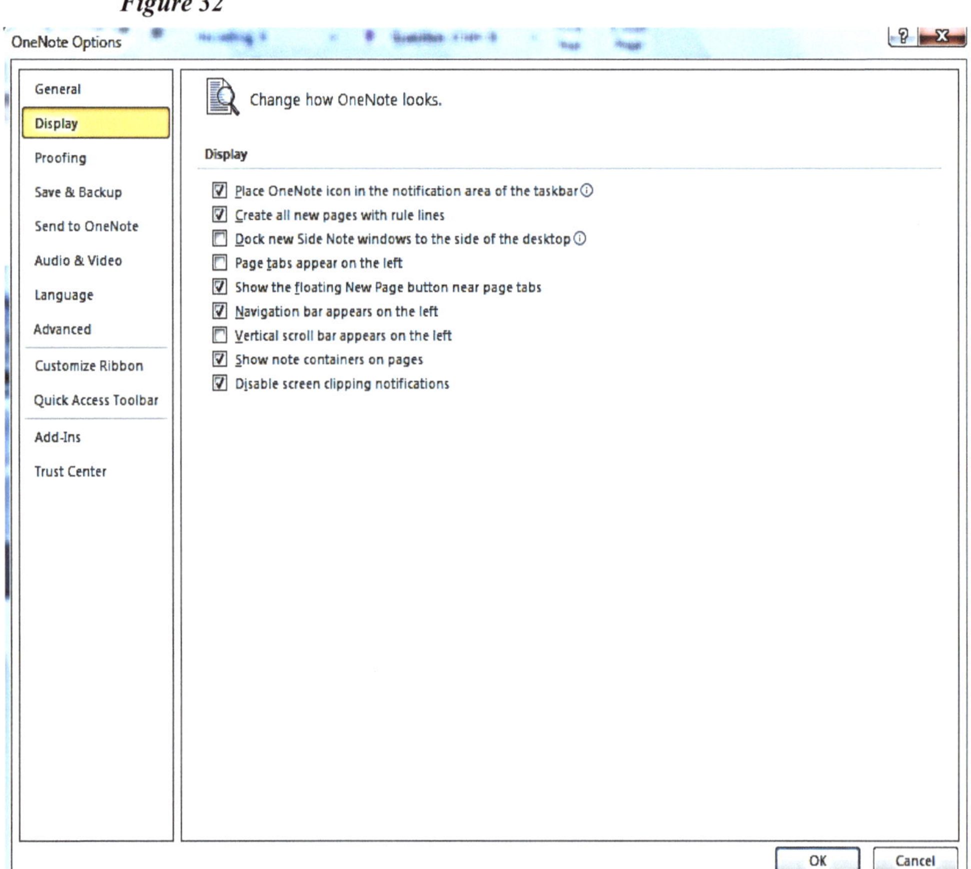

Proofing Options

Behind the Proofing Options dialog box you can see and change how OneNote corrects and formats your text. Here are a few basics to consider. First, if you are not familiar with the AutoCorrect feature available in Word, Excel and PowerPoint, take some time to explore this feature by clicking on the AutoCorrect Options button now. Notice that this feature is set-up by default to correct two initial capitals as well as capitalize the names of the days of the week. The default options are indicated by the check mark (✓). You can turn-on/off any of these options by clicking into the checkbox

The AutoCorrect database contains frequently misspelled and mistyped words, however you can add your own list of words by typing those words into the "Replace" and "With" fields.

Figure 33

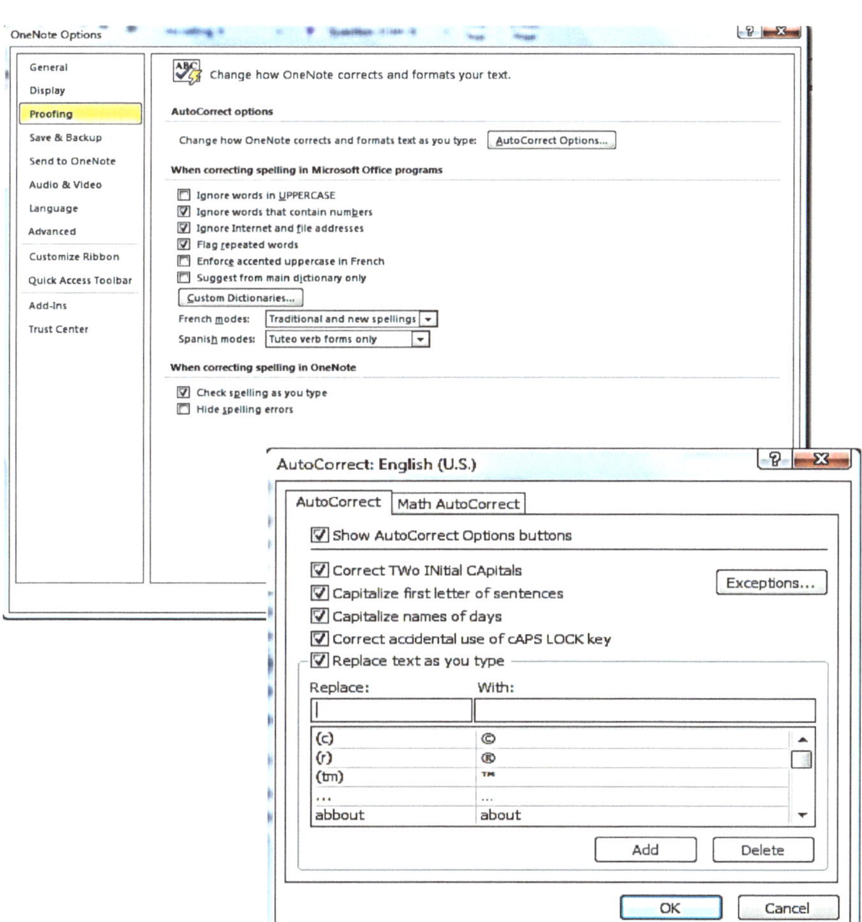

As you become more skilled at using OneNote, try experimenting with other AutoCorrect features, such as the Exceptions and Math AutoCorrect functions.

Save & Back-up

To customize how OneNote saves and backs up your files, you will want to look at the Save & Backup menu option. Pay particular attention to the Save section depicted in Figure 34. There you can see where your unified notes, backup folder and default notebook is being stored. Next, examine the Backup section, and notice you have the ability to regulate how often your notebooks are backed up. Of course, you can adjust the default setting based on your particular needs by selecting the drop-down list.

Finally, as the size of your notebook files increase, you may notice that it takes a little longer than usual for OneNote to open. For this reason, ensure that the Optimize files option is selected. See Figure 34 below.

Figure 34

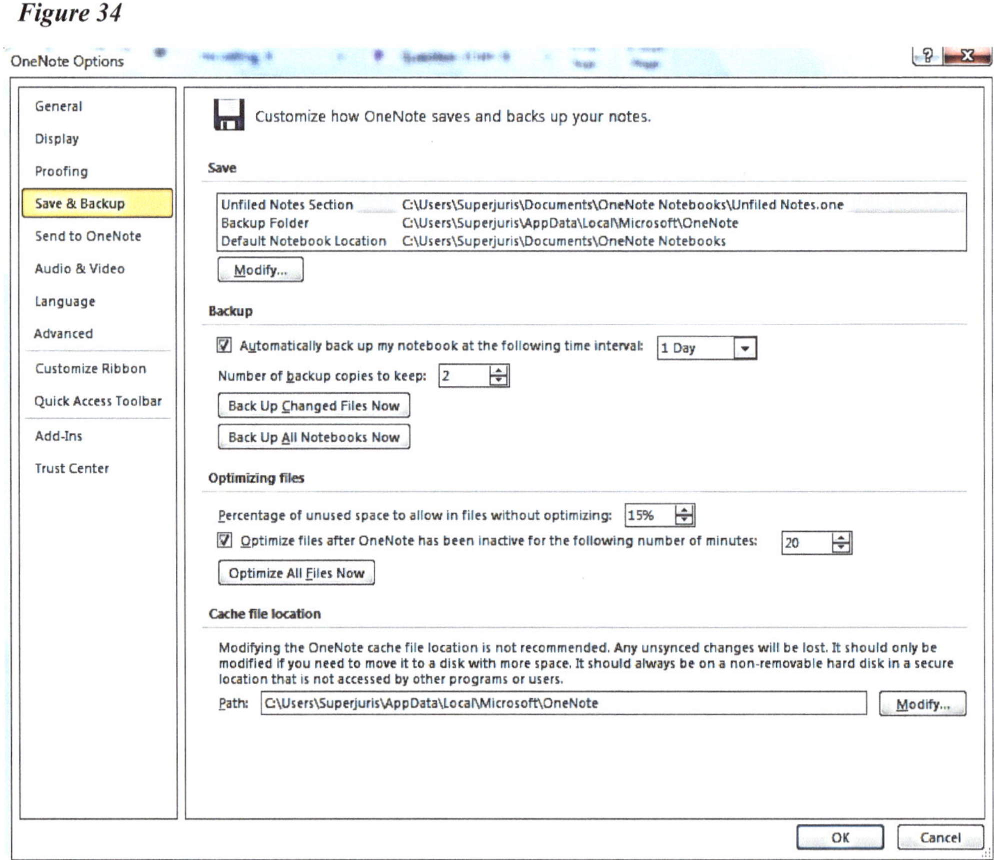

Customize the Ribbon

You can customize the OneNote Ribbon through this menu option. Here you can choose to add or delete commands. For example, if you do not have a need for the Time Stamp command, simply select it as we have in Figure 35, and then click on the Remove button.

Figure 35

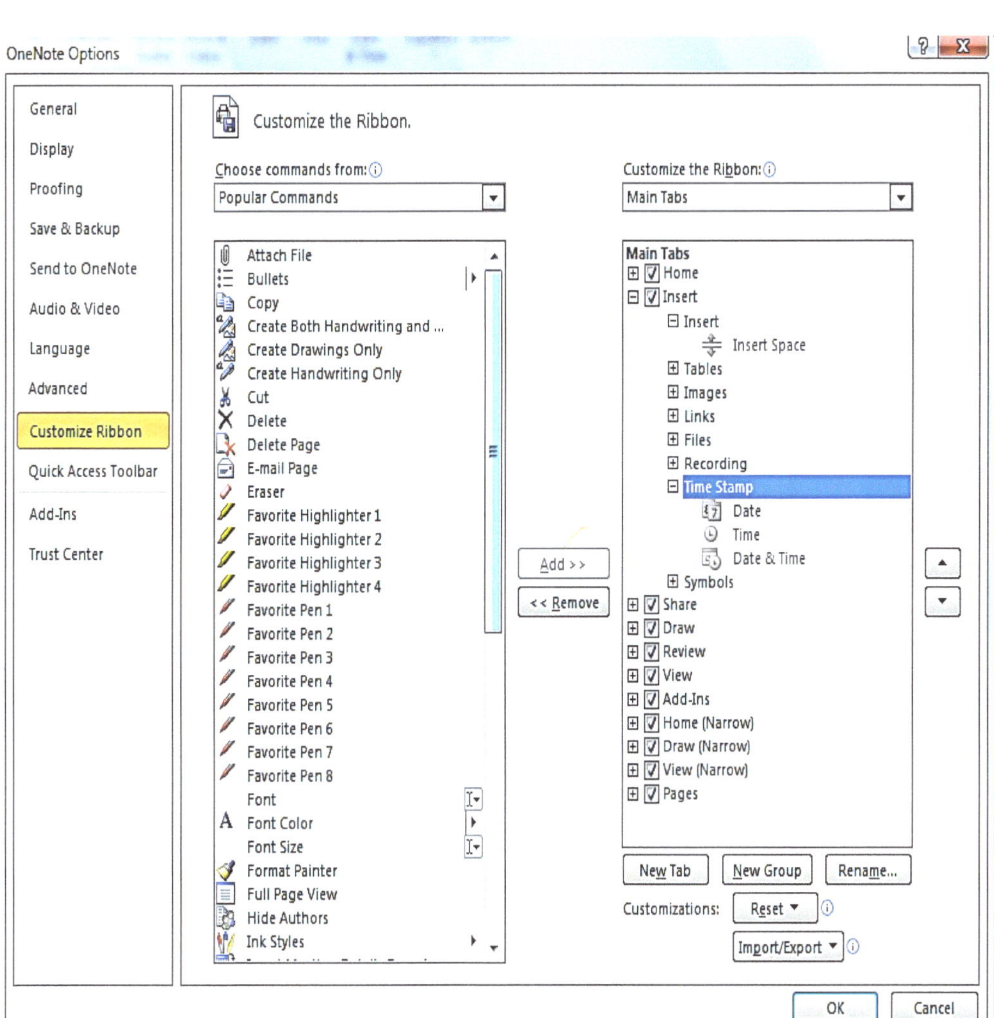

Linked Notes

One of the features you are sure to enjoy working with is called Linked Notes. Essentially, linked notes enables you to link your notebook to any other application you may have open such as Excel, Word, PowerPoint or the Internet OneNote anchors a notepad to the desktop that will remain on the screen as your work within other applications. You can copy and paste or drag and drop text from these applications into a OneNote page. See Figure 36.

Create Linked Notes

1. Click on the Review tab.
2. Click the Linked Notes button
3. Select the location (section or page) in which to put the item.
4. Open another application. A OneNote page is anchored to the desktop.

Figure 36

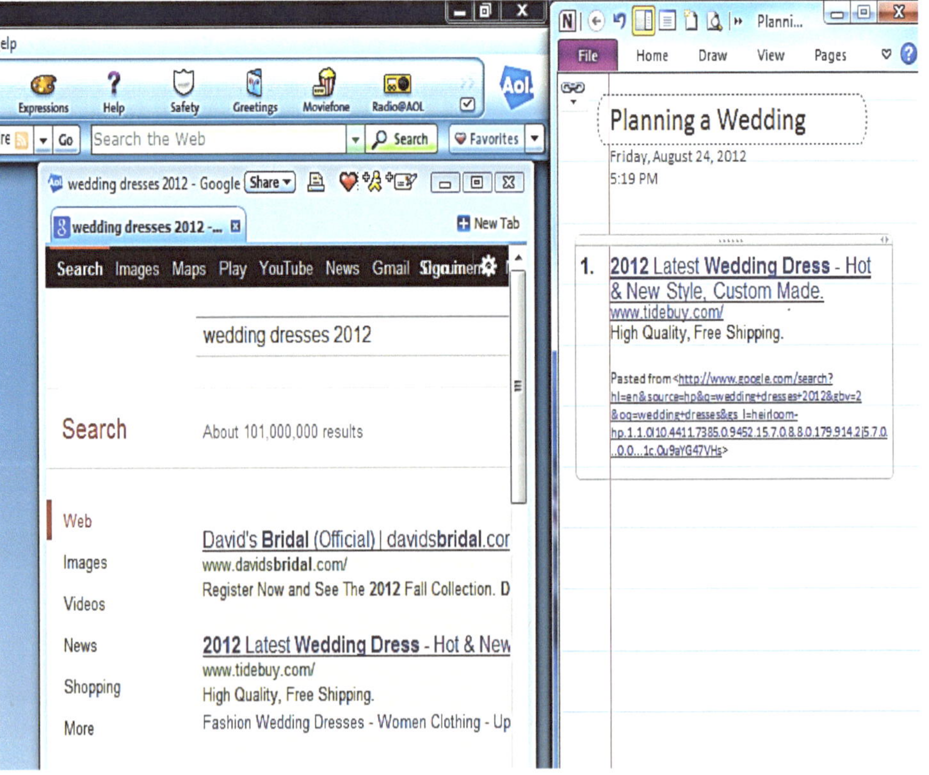

My Notes:

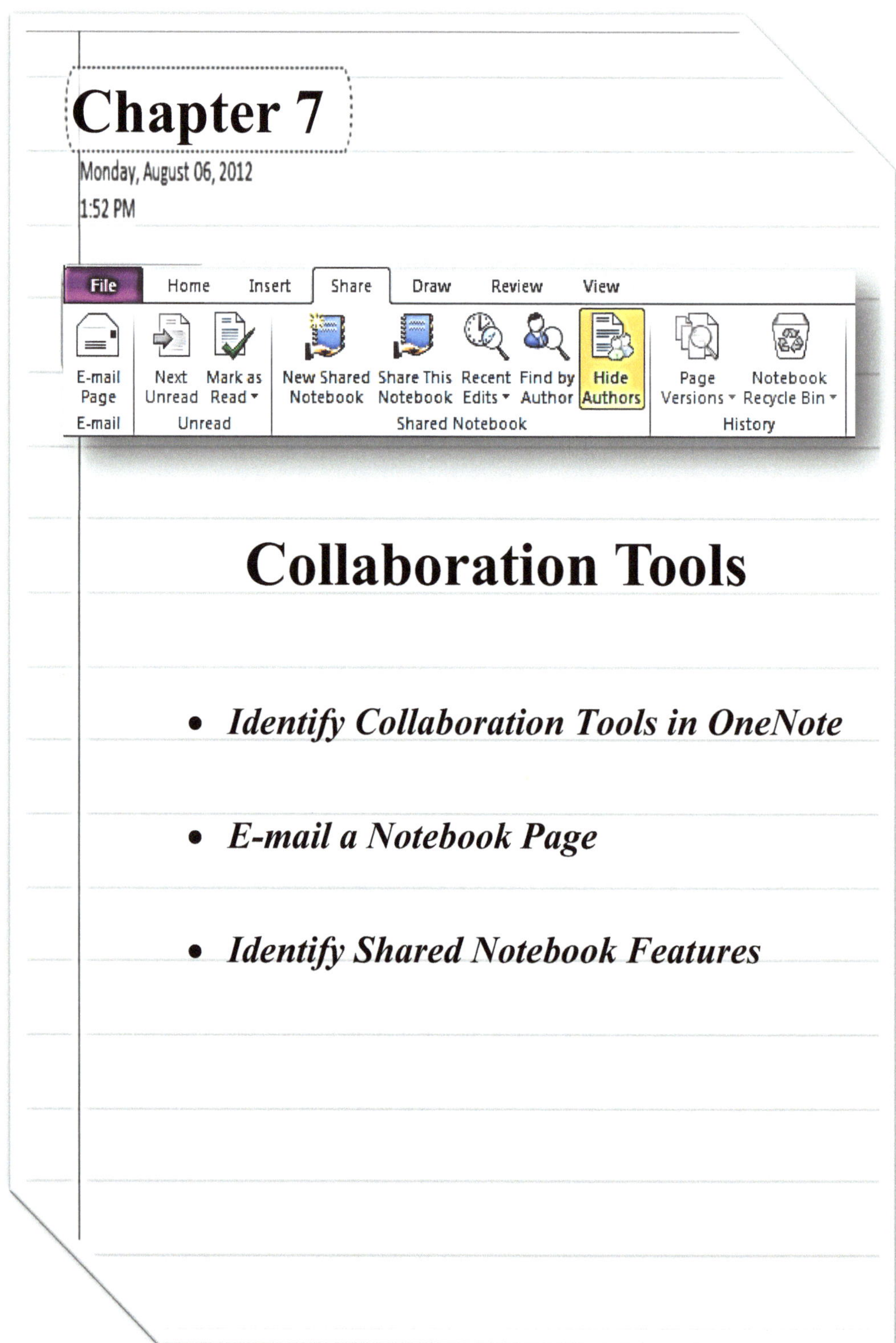

The estimated time required to complete all of these tasks is 5.5 minutes.

E-Mail a Notebook Page

Assume you have created some rather interesting notebook pages. Should you decide to share these pages, you will find one button makes the task very easy to do.

On OneNote's Share tab, you will find a single button within the E-mail group. When you click on the E-mail Page button, OneNote will attempt to e-mail the active page (where your cursor is located) through your personal or business e-mail account. You may find it easier to open your e-mail program before you select the E-mail Page button. Your notebook page is sent as an attached web page.

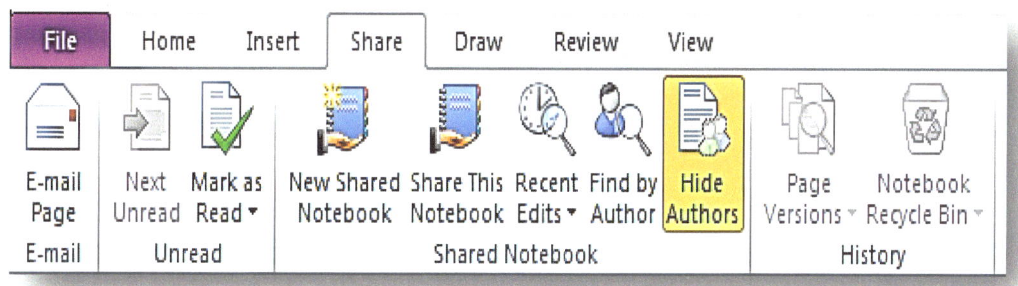

To E-Mail a Notebook Page

1. Open the notebook containing the page you wish to e-mail.
2. Click on the Share tab
3. Click on the E-mail Page button; your e-mail program should open.
4. Enter the addressee e-mail address.

⊠⊠⊠⊠⊠⊠⊠⊠⊠⊠⊠⊠⊠⊠⊠⊠⊠⊠⊠⊠⊠⊠⊠⊠⊠⊠⊠⊠⊠⊠

Shared Notebooks

Though the subject goes a little beyond the scope of this book, I thought it might be useful to explain a little about OneNote's Shared Notebook feature. Essentially, what you are doing through this feature is placing your files on the Web in a way that makes them accessible to others. OneNote makes it possible to share a notebook with friends or colleagues. In addition, you can also track edits made by others to shared notebooks as well as search for edits by other authors. You will find the Shared Notebook button on OneNote's Share tab. In order to share your notebook however, you will require a SharePoint account through your employer or you must obtain a personal Windows Live ID.

For more information regarding this feature, you will want to check out the Microsoft website or your system administrator at work.

Figure 37

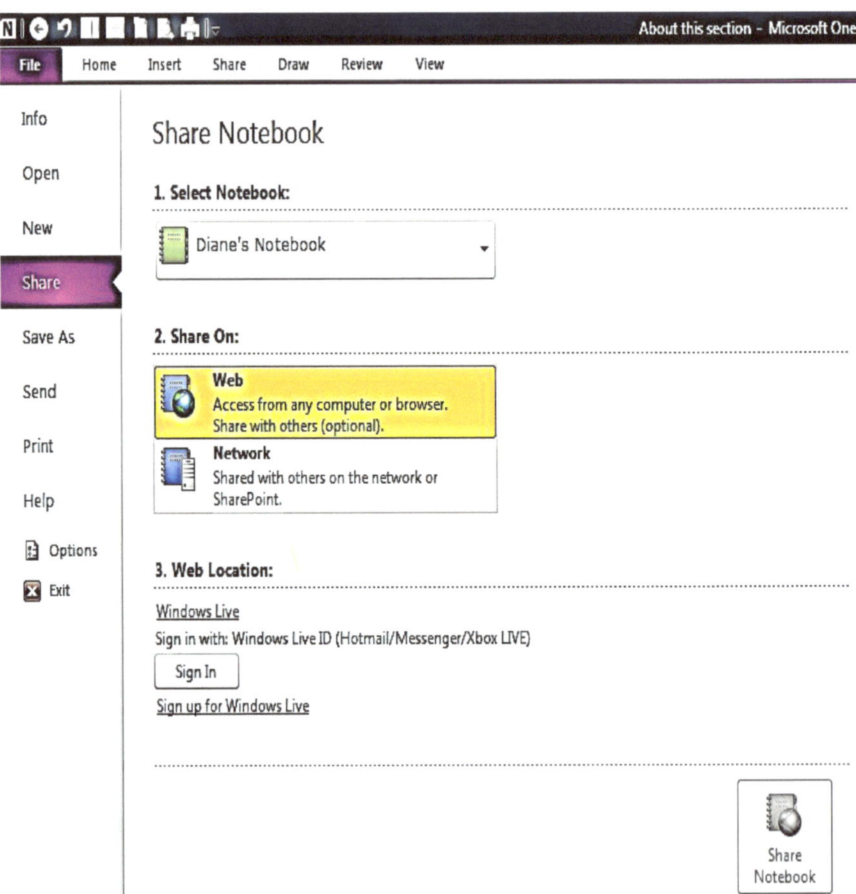

My Notes:

Chapter 8

Monday, August 06, 2012

1:52 PM

OneNote Ribbons & Tabs

- ***File Tab***
- ***Home Tab***
- ***Insert Tab***
- ***Share Tab***
- ***Drawing Tab***
- ***Review Tab***
- ***View Tab***

OneNote Ribbons & Tabs

The File Tab and Backstage View

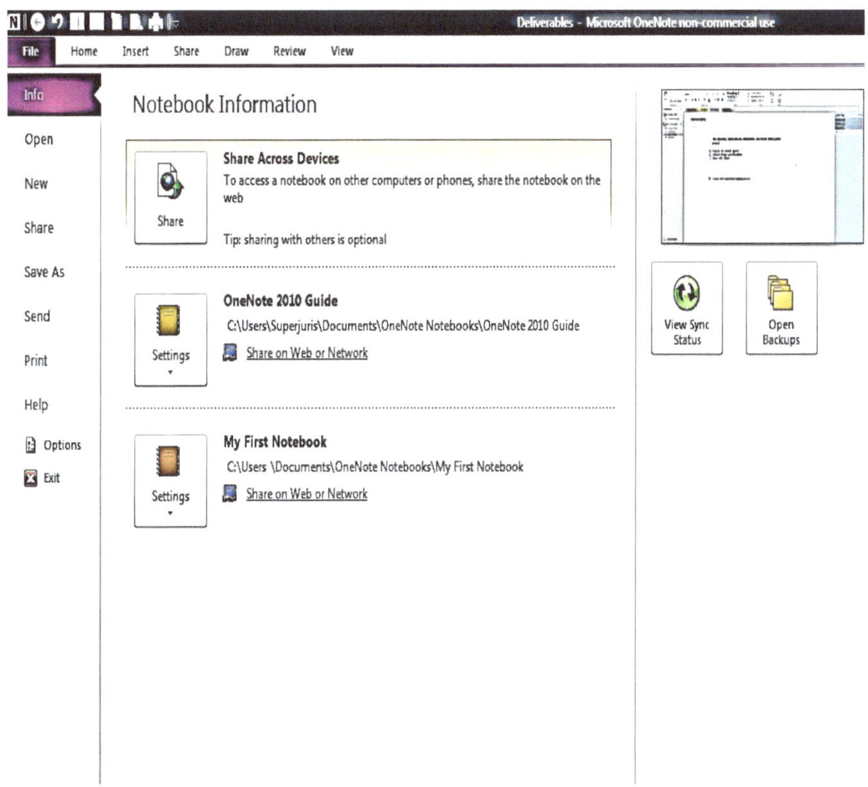

Figure 38

On the File tab, you will find a variety of menu options, such as Info, Open, Save As and Print. You can also exit from OneNote by using this menu.

Additionally, you will find online Help. If you need more information regarding a OneNote feature or function, you will find the online Help system very useful. Choose Options, if you want to customize the OneNote environment. For example, you can customize your ribbons, Autocorrect entries, and display preferences from the Options menu.

From the File tab, you may elect to share your notebook with others within your organization or externally.

OneNote Ribbons & Tabs

Home
On this ribbon, you will find useful tools for managing your notebook content. Notice the groups that reside on this ribbon such as Clipboard, Basic Text, Tags and Mail. You can use E-Mail Page to transmit a page within your notebook to friends or colleagues. You can also place a To Do tag within your notes to create a useful checkbox for task management.

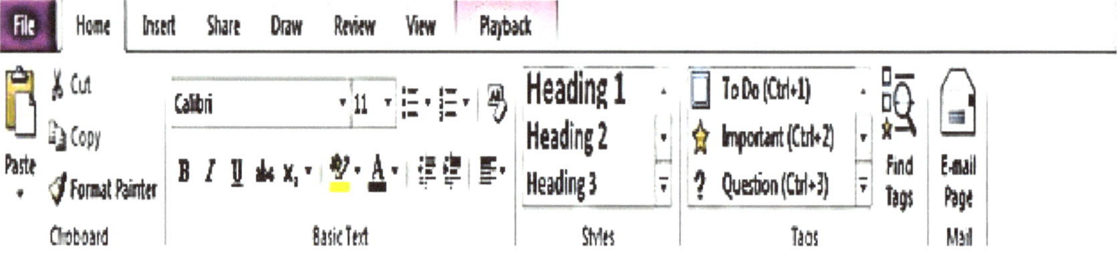

Insert
From the Insert tab you can place within your notes everything from a table to a video. Use the objects on this ribbon to record a meeting, your own narration or a video. You can also insert photographs into your notebook pages. Scanned and website images may also be inserted into your notebook.

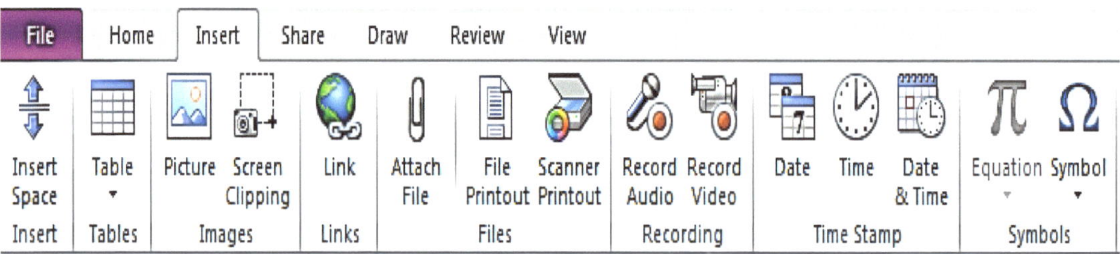

Share
Through OneNote, it is possible to collaborate and share your notebook with others. Create shared notebooks, e-mail specific pages, and track revisions.

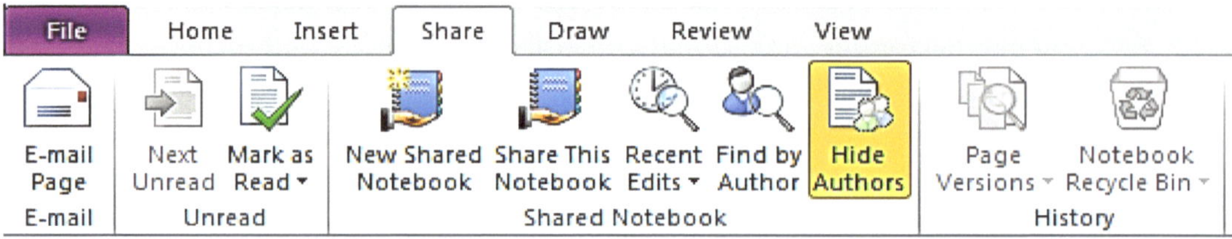

Drawing

Do you like to doodle in your notebook? On this ribbon, you will find a variety of free-hand drawing tools at your disposal. You can highlight text in your notebook just as you would do in hardcopy with OneNote's highlighter pens. You can also insert and color shapes.

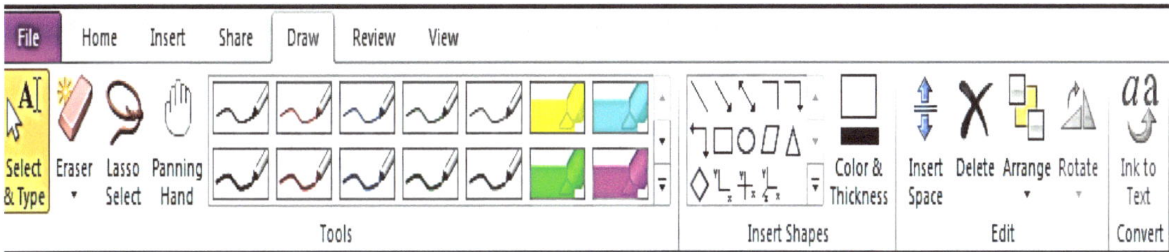

Review

OneNote makes it possible for you to not only create and edit notes, you can also check your spelling, do quick research of a subject on the Web or link notes in one notebook to another.

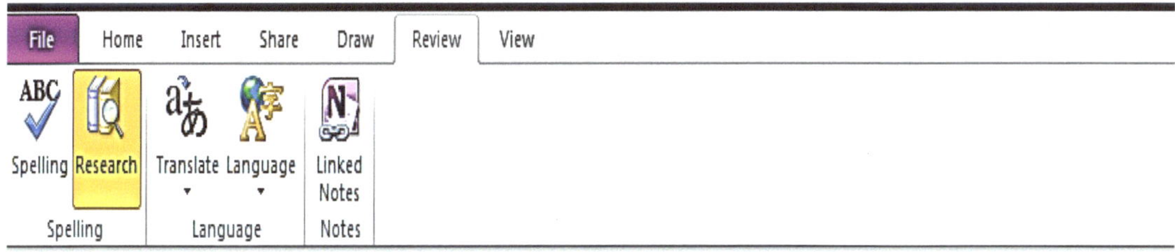

View

You can use the objects on the View tab handy for zooming in and out of your notebook. Enhance your notebook by applying rule lines to the page. In addition, you can change the color of your notebook pages and create side notes as temporary reminders.

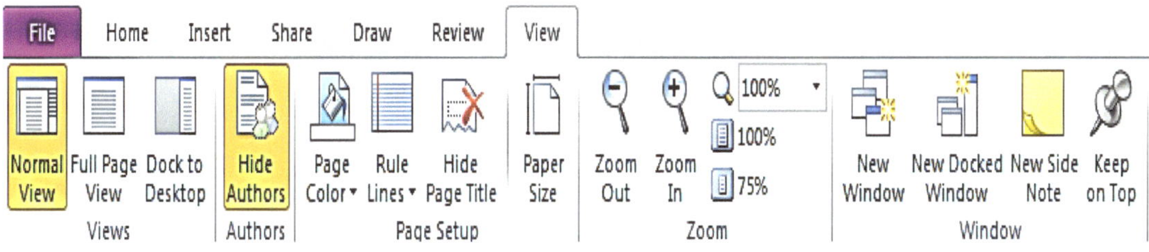

My Notes:

Online Resources

You will find a variety of helpful resources on the World Wide Web to assist you with Microsoft PowerPoint; below are just a few.

www.microsoft.com	➢ ***Access templates, tutorials and the latest updates concerning Microsoft Office applications and products.***
www.certiport.com	➢ *Use this portal to obtain information on how to become a certified Microsoft Office Specialist.*
www.mypcassociate.com	➢ *Obtain quick reference cards for Excel, Word, Outlook and PowerPoint. Find out about how you can learn new Microsoft applications.*
www.pcworld.com	➢ *Keep up to date with the latest software and hardware products on the market.*
http://www.pcmag.com/	➢ *Check out the PC Magazine web site for the latest news, downloads, deals and product reviews.*
http://magazine-directory.com/Smart-Computing.htm	➢ *Smart Computing is another great web site if you want to keep abreast of what is going on in the wonderful world of computers.*

My Notes:

INDEX

Table of Figures

About the Author

Diane Martin is executive director of My PC Associate NYC. She has been teaching computer applications in the fields of business and higher education since 1981. In 1999, with a background in business and legal technology, Diane migrated to the field of higher education, becoming the director of computer networking and support for a college of business and technology in New York City. She subsequently taught Computer Applications for Business at the DeVry Institute of Technology, and the Laboratory Institute of Merchandising, both in New York City. She is currently on the faculty of Continuing Education at Long Island University. Diane is a member of the Association of Information Technology Professionals and the Association of Women in Computing.

In addition to a Juris Doctor degree, Diane also holds a Master of Science degree in Instructional Technology from New York Institute of Technology, and a Bachelor of Arts degree in Liberal Arts from Long Island University. She is a certified Senior Professional in Human Resources, (SPHR) a certified Microsoft Office Specialist, and she holds a New York State Business School Teacher license.

My Notes:

My Notes:

My Notes:

www.ingramcontent.com/pod-product-compliance
Lightning Source LLC
Chambersburg PA
CBHW041421050326
40689CB00002B/606
9780985683740